Fodor's POCKET

savannah &
charleston

fifth edition

Excerpted from *Fodor's C*

fodor's travel publications
new york · toronto · london · sydney · auckland
www.fodors.com

contents

on the road with fodor's

A TRIP TAKES YOU OUT OF YOURSELF. Concerns of life at home disappear, driven away by more immediate thoughts—about, say, what marvels will beguile the next day, or where you'll have dinner. That's where Fodor's comes in. We make sure that you know all your options in Savannah and Charleston, so that you don't miss something that's around the next bend just because you didn't know it was there. Mindful that the best memories of your trip might have nothing to do with what you came to to see, we guide you to sights large and small. With Fodor's at your side, serendipitous discoveries are never far away.

Our success in showing you every corner of Savannah and Charleston is a credit to our extraordinary writers. They're the kind of people you'd poll for travel advice if you knew them. **Hollis Gillespie** was born in Southern California but moved to Atlanta in 1989 and almost immediately swapped her Valley Girl accent for a Southern drawl. A prolific travel writer and foreign-language interpreter, she writes a weekly humor column called "Mood Swings" for *Creative Loafing*, Atlanta's alternative newsweekly.

Charleston's **Mary Sue Lawrence** is a freelance writer and editor whose features on travel, entertainment, health, and business have appeared in national and British magazines. She is a South Carolina native and a proud descendant of General William

Moultrie. She lives in downtown Charleston, and is a frequent Fodor's contributor.

Don't Forget to Write

Your experiences—positive and negative—matter to us. If we have missed or misstated something, we want to hear about it. We follow up on all suggestions. Contact the Savannah and Charleston editors at editors@fodors.com or c/o Fodor's at 1745 Broadway, New York, NY 10019. And have a fabulous trip!

Karen Cure

Karen Cure
Editorial Director

the southeastern united states

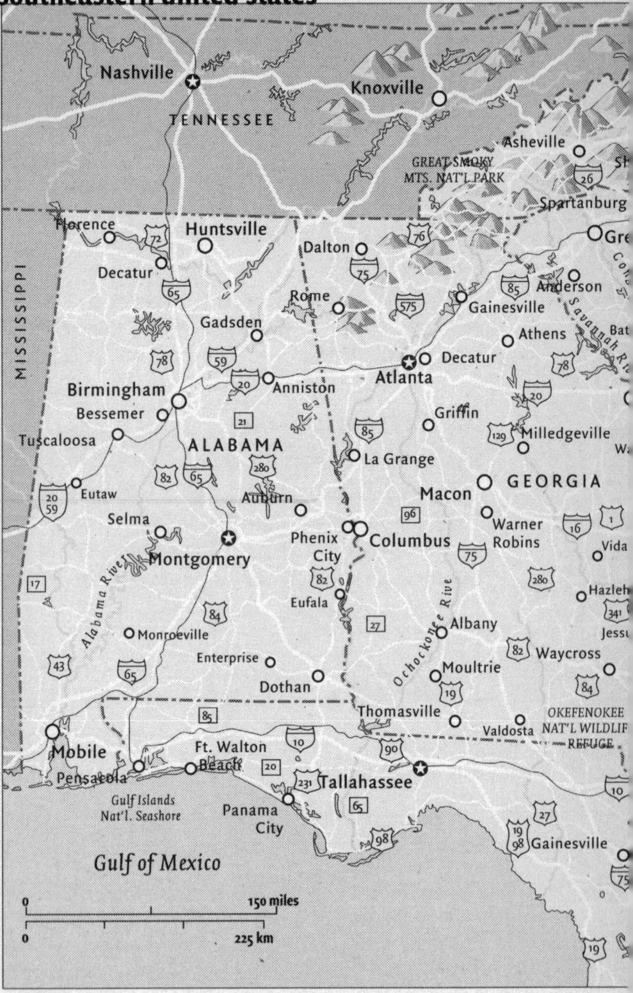

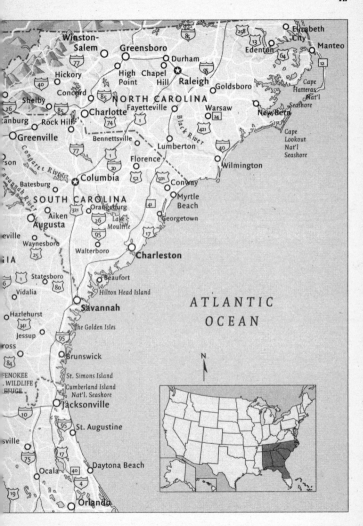

savannah &
charleston

introducing savannah and charleston

ONLY 108 MILES APART ALONG THE Atlantic coast, Savannah and Charleston share certain geographic characteristics and historical similarities, and are both gracious, well-preserved, and small. But although they may be sister cities, they're not identical twins.

Let's first get the clichés over with. Southern hospitality rules in both cities and both have beautiful mansions in a range of architectural styles, horse-drawn carriages clip-clopping on cobblestone streets, lovely gardens, oak trees dripping Spanish moss, and plenty of verandas on which to kick back with a mint julep. Both found wealth in their strategic locations on rivers with quick outlets to the Atlantic; Savannah is still the largest port between Baltimore and New Orleans and draws much of its wealth from port activity and shipbuilding. Both cities were at one time the capitals of their respective states. And both have long military histories. Charleston has Fort Sumter, where the first shots of the Civil War rang out, as well as the Citadel and a navy base. Savannah has Fort Jackson, Confederate headquarters of river batteries, and Fort Pulaski, captured by Union troops in 1862. And Sherman ended his march to the sea in Savannah in December 1864—the city was his Christmas present to Lincoln that year.

The first mark of difference between these two cities is, of course, that they're in different states. South Carolina is the smallest southern state while Georgia is the largest state east of the Mississippi. And it might surprise more than a few people that Savannah has a larger population than Charleston and that it throws the second-largest St. Patrick's Day celebration in the states (after New York City). But this does make sense, as Savannah is known to throw a good party. What sets Savannah apart from Charleston most of all is its squares. Savannah has the largest National Historic Landmark District (2½ square mi) in the United States. And oh, those verdant, picture-perfect, made-for-Hollywood squares surrounded by stately, exquisitely kept homes. The moss drips languorously, owners open their homes for tours, and visitors—most of whom have read John Berendt's 1994 best-seller *Midnight in the Garden of Good and Evil*—come. This is Berendt's take on the Savannah–Charleston rivalry:

Savannahians like to talk about Charleston most of all, especially in the presence of a newcomer. They would compare the two cities endlessly. Savannah was the Hostess City; Charleston was the Holy City (because it had a lot of churches). Savannah's streetscape was superior to Charleston's but Charleston had finer interiors. Savannah was thoroughly English in style and temperament; Charleston had French and Spanish influences as well as English. Savannah preferred hunting, fishing, and going to parties over intellectual pursuits; in Charleston it was the other way around. Savannah was attractive to tourists; Charleston was overrun by them. On and on. In the minds of most Americans, Savannah and Charleston were sister cities. If so, the sisters were barely on speaking terms. Savannahians rarely went to Charleston, even though it was less than two hours away by car. But then Savannahians rarely went anywhere at all. They could not be bothered. They were content to remain in their isolated city under self-imposed house arrest.

Well, several things have changed since the book's publication, most notably the part about Charleston attracting more visitors. Savannah's profile has been raised pronouncedly by Berendt's book and the subsequent movie version directed by Clint Eastwood and starring Kevin Spacey and John Cusack. But Charlestonians are taking all this fanfare in stride. They know they are not in danger of complete desertion. They host the wonderful Spoleto Festival USA of the arts every summer, and they have some of the best restaurants in the South, the most historic inns in the vicinity, and 181 churches. (Lest you think they are teetotalling holy rollers, you should know that it was a Charlestonian who invented Planter's punch.)

Eminently beautiful and strollable, Charleston and Savannah give each other a run for their money. (A little sibling rivalry never hurt anyone.) Compare for yourself.

IN THIS CHAPTER

Updated by Hollis Gillespie

savannah

THE VERY SOUND OF THE NAME *Savannah* conjures up misty images of mint juleps, handsome mansions, and a somewhat decadent city moving at a lazy Southern pace. It's hard even to say "Savannah" without drawling. Well, brace yourself. The mint juleps are there all right, along with the moss and the mansions and the easygoing pace, but this Southern belle rings with surprises. Take, for example, St. Patrick's Day: Savannah has a St. Patrick's Day celebration second only to New York's. The greening of Savannah began in 1812, and everybody in town talks a blue (green) streak about St. Patrick's Day. Everything turns green on March 17, including scrambled eggs and grits.

Savannah's modern history began on February 12, 1733, when English general James Edward Oglethorpe and 120 colonists arrived at Yamacraw Bluff on the Savannah River to found the 13th and last colony in the New World. As the port city grew, people from England and Ireland, Scottish Highlanders, French Huguenots, Germans, Austrian Salzburgers, Sephardic and Ashkenazic Jews, Moravians, Italians, Swiss, Welsh, and Greeks all arrived to create what could be called a rich gumbo.

In 1793 Eli Whitney of Connecticut, who was tutoring on a plantation near Savannah, invented a mechanized means of "ginning" seeds from cotton bolls. Cotton soon became king, and Savannah, already a busy seaport, flourished under its reign. Waterfront warehouses were filled with "white gold," and brokers trading in the Savannah Cotton Exchange set world prices. The white gold brought in solid gold, and fine mansions were built in the prospering city.

In 1864 Savannahians surrendered their city to Union general Sherman rather than see it torched. Later, following World War I and the decline of the cotton market, the city's economy virtually collapsed, and its historic buildings languished for more than 30 years. Elegant mansions were razed or allowed to decay, and cobwebs replaced cotton in the dilapidated riverfront warehouses.

In 1955 Savannah's spirits rose again. News that the exquisite Isaiah Davenport House (324 E. State St.) was to be destroyed prompted seven outraged ladies to raise money to buy the house. They saved it the day before the wrecking ball was to swing. Thus was born the Historic Savannah Foundation, the organization responsible for the restoration of downtown Savannah, where more than 1,000 restored buildings form the 2½-square-mi Historic District, the nation's largest. Many of these buildings are open to the public during the annual tour of homes, and today Savannah is one of the country's top 10 cities for walking tours.

John Berendt's wildly popular *Midnight in the Garden of Good and Evil* has lured many people to Savannah since the book's publication in 1994. A nonfiction account of a notorious 1980s shooting, the book brings to life such Savannah sites as Monterey Square, Mercer House, and Bonaventure Cemetery. Clint Eastwood's film adaptation, only loosely based on the book, was neither a box-office nor a critical success, but the public's interest in Savannah has remained intense—to the consternation of old-timers who find the story's characters less than savory and the nosy Northerners a nuisance. Other Savannahians have rolled out the welcome mat, while still others have hiked prices, profiting from the tourist dollars.

HERE AND THERE

Georgia's founder, General James Oglethorpe, laid out the city on a perfect grid. The Historic District is neatly hemmed in by the Savannah River, Gaston Street, East Street, and Martin Luther King Jr. Boulevard. Streets are arrow-straight, public squares of varying sizes are tucked into the grid at precise intervals, and each block is sliced in half by narrow, often unpaved streets. Bull Street, anchored on the north by City Hall and the south by Forsyth Park, charges down the center of the grid and lunges around the five public squares that stand in its way.

THE HISTORIC DISTRICT

Numbers in the text correspond to numbers in the margin and on the Savannah Historic District map.

A Good Walk and Drive

You can cover historic Savannah on foot, but to save time and energy, you might want to drive part of this tour. Start at the **SAVANNAH VISITORS CENTER** ①, on Martin Luther King Jr. Boulevard. In the same building, the **SAVANNAH HISTORY MUSEUM** ② is an ideal introduction to the city's history. There is public parking next to the center and museum.

Exit the parking lot and turn left (north), walking or driving two short and one very long blocks on Martin Luther King Jr. Boulevard to the **SCARBOROUGH HOUSE** ③, which contains the Ships of the Sea Museum. Cross Martin Luther King Jr. Boulevard and continue two blocks east on West Congress Street, past Franklin Square to **CITY MARKET** ④. Skirting around Franklin Square north on Montgomery Street, go two blocks to West Bay Street and turn right.

savannah historic district

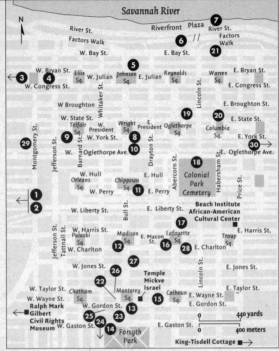

Savannah River

From this point continue east on West Bay Street four blocks to Bull Street. On your left you'll see **CITY HALL** ⑤. Continue east along West Bay Street (which now becomes East Bay Street) to **FACTORS WALK** ⑥, which lies south of River Street and the Savannah River. If you're driving, leave your car here to continue on foot (be sure to choose long-term parking, as the short-term meters are monitored vigilantly). Step down from Factors Walk toward the river and visit **RIVERFRONT PLAZA** ⑦, which is best seen on foot.

At this point, if you're driving, you'll probably want to get back in your car to continue the tour. Return to East Bay Street and head west two long blocks back to Bull Street. Walk four blocks south on Bull Street to **WRIGHT SQUARE** ⑧; then turn right (west) and go two blocks to Telfair Square, where you can stop at the **TELFAIR MANSION AND ART MUSEUM** ⑨. Stroll around Telfair Square and then continue east on West York Street back toward Wright Square, and turn right on Bull Street, heading two blocks south to the **JULIETTE GORDON LOW BIRTHPLACE/GIRL SCOUT NATIONAL CENTER** ⑩. Two more short blocks south from the Low House on Bull Street, and you'll reach **CHIPPEWA SQUARE** ⑪. Continue south on Bull Street to the Gothic Revival **GREEN-MELDRIM HOUSE** ⑫. Next, walk four blocks south on Bull Street to **MONTEREY SQUARE** ⑬. Proceed two blocks farther south from Monterey Square to **FORSYTH PARK** ⑭, the divide between East and West Gaston streets.

From the park walk east on East Gaston Street and go one block to Abercorn Street; then turn left (north) on Abercorn Street to Calhoun Square and note the **WESLEY MONUMENTAL CHURCH** ⑮. Continue north on Abercorn four blocks to Lafayette Square and view the **ANDREW LOW HOUSE** ⑯. Northeast of Lafayette Square looms the **CATHEDRAL OF ST. JOHN THE BAPTIST** ⑰, on East Harris Street. Two blocks north, at the intersection of Abercorn and East Oglethorpe streets, is the huge **COLONIAL PARK CEMETERY** ⑱. Proceeding two blocks north on Abercorn Street from the cemetery takes you to Oglethorpe Square; across from the square is the **OWENS-THOMAS HOUSE AND MUSEUM** ⑲. From the house walk east on East President Street two blocks to Columbia Square. Northwest of the square on East State Street stands the **ISAIAH DAVENPORT HOUSE** ⑳. From here continue north up Habersham Street to **EMMET PARK** ㉑, a splendid park to relax in at the end of your tour.

TIMING

This is a long but comfortable walk, as Savannah has no taxing hills. Allow a full day to see everything along this route, especially if you plan to read all the historic markers and explore the sights thoroughly, stopping for tours. Driving around the squares can be slow—but you can drive the entire route in two hours, a pace that allows for some stopping along the way. Allow extra time if you want to linger in Riverfront Plaza for a half hour or so.

What to See

⑯ ANDREW LOW HOUSE. This residence was built in 1848 for Andrew Low, a native of Scotland and one of Savannah's merchant princes. The home later belonged to his son William, who married Juliette Gordon. After her husband's death, she founded the Girl Scouts in this house on March 12, 1912. The house has 19th-century antiques, stunning silver, and some of the finest ornamental ironwork in Savannah. *329 Abercorn St., Historic District, tel. 912/233–6854, www.andrewlow.com. $7. Mon.–Wed. and Fri.–Sat. 10:30–3:30, Sun. noon–3:30.*

BEACH INSTITUTE AFRICAN-AMERICAN CULTURAL CENTER. It's in the building that housed the first school for African-American children in Savannah, established after emancipation (1867). The center exhibits works by African-American artists from the Savannah area and around the country. *502 E. Harris*

St., Historic District, tel. 912/234–8000, www.kingtisdell.org/beach. $3.50. Tues.–Sat. noon–5.

⑰ CATHEDRAL OF ST. JOHN THE BAPTIST. Soaring over the city, the French Gothic–style cathedral, with pointed arches and free-flowing traceries, is the seat of the diocese of Savannah. It was founded in 1799 by the first French colonists to arrive in Savannah. Fire destroyed the early structures; the present cathedral dates from 1874. *222 E. Harris St., Historic District, tel. 912/233–4709. Weekdays 9–5.*

⑪ CHIPPEWA SQUARE. Daniel Chester French's imposing bronze statue of General James Edward Oglethorpe, founder of Savannah and Georgia, anchors the square. Also note the **Savannah Theatre**, on Bull Street, which claims to be the oldest continuously operated theater site in North America. *Bull St. between Hull and Perry Sts., Historic District.*

⑤ CITY HALL. Built in 1905 on the site of the Old City Exchange (1799–1904), this imposing structure anchors Bay Street. Notice the bench commemorating Oglethorpe's landing on February 12, 1733. *1 Bay St., Historic District, tel. 912/651–6410. Weekdays 8–5.*

④ CITY MARKET. Alas, the original 1870s City Market was razed years ago to make way for a dreary-looking parking garage. Next to the garage you'll find this popular pedestrians-only area that encompasses galleries, nightclubs, restaurants, and shops. *Between Franklin Sq. and Johnson Sq. on W. St. Julian St., Historic District.*

★ **⑱ COLONIAL PARK CEMETERY.** The park is the final resting place for Savannahians who died between 1750 and 1853. You may want to stroll the shaded pathways and read some of the old tombstone inscriptions. There are several historical plaques, one of which marks the grave of Button Gwinnett, a signer of the Declaration of Independence. *Oglethorpe and Abercorn Sts., Historic District.*

COLUMBIA SQUARE. When Savannah was a walled city (1757–90), Bethesda Gate (one of six) was here. The square was laid out in 1799. *Habersham St. between E. State and E. York Sts., Historic District.*

㉑ EMMET PARK. The lovely tree-shaded park is named for Robert Emmet, a late-18th-century Irish patriot and orator. *Borders E. Bay St., Historic District.*

❻ FACTORS WALK. A network of iron walkways connects Bay Street with the multistory buildings that rise up from the river level, and iron stairways descend from Bay Street to Factors Walk. Cobblestone ramps lead pedestrians down to River Street (these are serious cobblestones, so wear comfortable shoes). *Bay St. to Factors Walk, Historic District.*

⓮ FORSYTH PARK. The park forms the southern border of Bull Street. On its 20 acres it has a glorious white fountain dating to 1858, Confederate and Spanish-American War memorials, and the Fragrant Garden for the Blind, a project of Savannah garden clubs. There are tennis courts and a tree-shaded jogging path. Outdoor plays and concerts often take place here. At the northwest corner of the park, in **Hodgson Hall**, a 19th-century Italianate–Greek Revival building, you'll find the **Georgia Historical Society**, which shows selections from its collection of artifacts and manuscripts. *501 Whitaker St., Historic District, tel. 912/651–2128, www.georgiahistory.com. Tues.–Sat. 10–5.*

★ ⓬ GREEN-MELDRIM HOUSE. Designed by New York architect John Norris and built in 1850 for cotton merchant Charles Green, this Gothic Revival mansion cost $90,000 to build—a princely sum back then. The house was bought in 1892 by Judge Peter Meldrim, whose heirs sold it to **St. John's Episcopal Church** to use as a parish house. General Sherman lived here after taking the city in 1864. Sitting on **Madison Square,** the house has such Gothic features as a crenellated roof, oriels, and an external gallery with filigree ironwork. Inside are mantels of Carrara marble, carved blackwalnut woodwork, and doorknobs and hinges of either silver plate or porcelain. 1 W. Macon St., Historic District, tel. 912/233–3845. $5. Tues., Thurs., and Fri. 10–4, Sat. 10–1. Closed last 2 wks of Jan. and 2 wks before Easter.

★ ⑳ **ISAIAH DAVENPORT HOUSE.** The proposed demolition of this historic Savannah structure galvanized the city's residents into action to save their treasured buildings. Semicircular stairs with wrought-iron trim lead to the recessed doorway of the redbrick federal mansion that master builder Isaiah Davenport built for himself between 1815 and 1820. Three dormer windows poke through the sloping roof of the stately house, and the interior has polished hardwood floors, fine woodwork and plasterwork, and a soaring elliptical staircase. Furnishings, from the 1820s, are Hepplewhite, Chippendale, and Sheraton. 324 E. State St., Historic District, tel. 912/236–8097, www.davenportsavga.com. $7. Mon.–Sat. 10–4, Sun. 1–4.

JOHNSON SQUARE. The oldest of James Oglethorpe's original 24 squares was laid out in 1733 and named for South Carolina governor Robert Johnson. A monument marks the grave of Nathanael Greene, a hero of the Revolutionary War. The square was once a popular gathering place: Savannahians came here to welcome President Monroe in 1819, to greet the Marquis de Lafayette in 1825, and to cheer for Georgia's secession in 1861. Bull St. between Bryan and Congress Sts., Historic District.

⑩ **JULIETTE GORDON LOW BIRTHPLACE/GIRL SCOUT NATIONAL CENTER.** This majestic Regency town house, attributed to William Jay (built 1818–21), was designated in 1965 as Savannah's first National Historic Landmark. "Daisy" Low, founder of the Girl Scouts, was born here in 1860, and the house is now owned and operated by the Girl Scouts of America. Mrs. Low's paintings and other artwork are on display in the house, restored to the style of 1886, the year of Mrs. Low's marriage. 142 Bull St., Historic District, tel. 912/233–4501, www.girlscouts.org/birthplace. $8. Mon.– Tues. and Thurs.–Sat. 10–4, Sun. 12:30–4:30.

OFF THE
BEATEN
PATH **KING-TISDELL COTTAGE** – Tucked behind a picket fence is this museum dedicated to the preservation of African-American history and culture. The Negro Heritage Trail Tour visits this little Victorian house. Broad steps lead to a porch, and dormer windows pop up through a steep roof. The interior is furnished to resemble a middle-class African-American coastal home of the 1890s. To reach the cottage by car, go east on East Bay Street to Price Street and turn south (right) on this street; continue for about 30 blocks to East Huntington Street and take a left (east). The building is in the middle of the block. *514 E. Huntington St., Historic District, tel. 912/234–8000, www.kingtisdell.org. $3.50. By appointment.*

LAFAYETTE SQUARE. Named for the Marquis de Lafayette, the square contains a graceful three-tier fountain donated by the Georgia chapter of the Colonial Dames of America. *Abercorn St. between E. Harris and E. Charlton Sts., Historic District.*

MADISON SQUARE. A statue on the square, laid out in 1839 and named for President James Madison, depicts Sergeant William Jasper hoisting a flag and is a tribute to his bravery during the Siege of Savannah. Though mortally wounded, Jasper rescued the colors of his regiment in the assault on the British lines. *Bull St. between W. Harris and W. Charlton Sts., Historic District.*

⓭ MONTEREY SQUARE. Commemorating the victory of General Zachary Taylor's forces in Monterrey, Mexico, in 1846, this is the fifth and southernmost of Bull Street's squares. A monument honors General Casimir Pulaski, the Polish nobleman who lost his life in the Siege of Savannah during the Revolutionary War. Also on the square is Temple Mickve Israel. *Bull St. between Taylor and Gordon Sts., Historic District.*

★ ⓳ OWENS-THOMAS HOUSE AND MUSEUM. English architect William Jay's first Regency mansion in Savannah is the city's finest example of that architectural style. Built in 1816–19, the

English house was constructed mostly with local materials. Of particular note are the curving walls of the house, Greek-inspired ornamental molding, half-moon arches, stained-glass panels, and Duncan Phyfe furniture. In 1825 the Marquis de Lafayette bade a two-hour au revoir from a wrought-iron balcony to a crowd below. *124 Abercorn St., Historic District, tel. 912/233–9743, www.telfair.org. $8. Mon. noon–5, Tues.–Sat. 10–5, Sun. 1–5.*

OFF THE BEATEN PATH

RALPH MARK GILBERT CIVIL RIGHTS MUSEUM – In Savannah's Historic District, this history museum has a series of 15 exhibits on segregation, from emancipation through the civil rights movement. The role of black and white Savannahians in ending segregation in their city is detailed in these exhibits, largely derived from archival photographs. The museum also has touring exhibits. *460 Martin Luther King Jr. Blvd., Historic District, tel. 912/231–8900, fax 912/234–2577. $4. Mon.–Sat. 9–5.*

REYNOLDS SQUARE. John Wesley, who preached in Savannah and wrote the first English hymnal in the city in 1736, is remembered here. A monument to the founder of the Methodist Church is shaded by greenery and surrounded by park benches. The **Olde Pink House** (23 Abercorn St., Historic District), built in 1771, is one of the oldest buildings in town. Now a restaurant, the porticoed pink-stucco Georgian mansion has been a private home, a bank, and headquarters for a Yankee general during the Civil War. *Abercorn St. between E. Bryant and E. Congress Sts., Historic District.*

⑦ RIVERFRONT PLAZA. Here you can watch a parade of freighters and pug-nose tugs; youngsters can play in the tugboat-shape sandboxes. River Street is the main venue for many of the city's celebrations, including the First Saturday festivals, when flea marketers, artists, and artisans display their wares and musicians entertain the crowds. *River St. between Abercorn and Barnard St., Historic District.*

❷ SAVANNAH HISTORY MUSEUM. This museum in a restored railway station is an excellent introduction to the city. Exhibits range from old locomotives to a tribute to Savannah-born songwriter Johnny Mercer. On top of the **site of the Siege of Savannah,** it marks the spot where in 1779 the colonial forces, led by Polish count Casimir Pulaski, laid siege to Savannah in an attempt to retake the city from the redcoats. They were beaten back, and Pulaski was killed while leading a cavalry charge against the British. The dead lie underneath the building. *303 Martin Luther King Jr. Blvd., Historic District, tel. 912/238–1779, www.chsgeorgia.org/historymuseum.cfm. $4. Daily 9–5.*

❶ SAVANNAH VISITORS CENTER. Come here for free maps and brochures, friendly advice, and an audiovisual overview of the city. The starting point for a number of guided tours, the center is in a big 1860 redbrick building with high ceilings and sweeping arches. It was the old Central of Georgia railway station. The parking lot is a good spot to leave your car while you explore the nearby Historic District. *301 Martin Luther King Jr. Blvd., Historic District, tel. 912/944–0455, www.savannahvisit.com. Weekdays 8:30–5, weekends 9–5.*

❸ SCARBOROUGH HOUSE. This exuberant Greek Revival mansion, built during the 1819 cotton boom for Savannah merchant prince William Scarborough, was designed by English architect William Jay. Scarborough was a major investor in the steamship *Savannah.* The house has a Doric portico capped by one of Jay's characteristic half-moon windows. Four massive Doric columns form a peristyle in the atrium entrance hall. Inside is the **Ships of the Sea Museum,** with displays of ship models, including steamships, a nuclear-powered ship (the *Savannah*), China clippers with their sails unfurled, and Columbus's vessels. *41 Martin Luther King Jr. Blvd., Historic District, tel. 912/232–1511, www.shipsofthesea.org. $5. Tues.–Sun. 10–5.*

❾ TELFAIR MANSION AND ART MUSEUM. The oldest public art museum in the Southeast was designed by William Jay in 1819 for

Alexander Telfair and sits across the street from **Telfair Square.** Within its marble rooms are American, French, and Dutch impressionist paintings; German tonalist paintings; a large collection of works by Kahlil Gibran; plaster casts of the Elgin Marbles, the Venus de Milo, and the Laocoön, among other classical sculptures; and some of the Telfair family furnishings, including a Duncan Phyfe sideboard and Savannah-made silver. *121 Barnard St., Historic District, tel.* 912/232–1177, *www.telfair.org.* $8, *free Sun. Mon. noon–5, Tues.–Sat.* 10–5, *Sun.* 1–5.

TEMPLE MICKVE ISRAEL. A Gothic Revival synagogue on Monterey Square houses the third-oldest Jewish congregation in the United States; its founding members settled in town five months after the establishment of Savannah in 1733. The synagogue's collection includes documents and letters (some from George Washington, James Madison, and Thomas Jefferson) pertaining to early Jewish life in Savannah and Georgia. *20 E. Gordon St., Historic District, tel.* 912/233–1547, *www.mickveisrael.org. Weekdays* 10–noon *and* 2–4.

⑮ **WESLEY MONUMENTAL CHURCH.** This Gothic Revival–style church memorializing the founders of Methodism is patterned after Queen's Kerk in Amsterdam. Noted for its magnificent stained-glass windows, the church celebrated a century of service in 1968. *429 Abercorn St., Historic District, tel.* 912/232–0191. *By appointment only.*

⑧ **WRIGHT SQUARE.** Named for James Wright, Georgia's last colonial governor, the square has an elaborate monument in its center that honors William Washington Gordon, founder of the Central of Georgia Railroad. A slab of granite from Stone Mountain adorns the grave of Tomo-Chi-Chi, the Yamacraw chief who befriended General Oglethorpe and the colonists. *Bull St. between W. State and W. York Sts., Historic District.*

MIDNIGHT IN THE GARDEN OF GOOD AND EVIL

Town gossips can give you the best introduction to a city, and as author John Berendt discovered, Savannah's not short on them. In his 1994 best-seller, *Midnight in the Garden of Good and Evil*, Berendt shares the juiciest of tales imparted to him during the eight years he spent here wining and dining with Savannah's high society and dancing with her Grand Empress, drag queen the Lady Chablis, among others. By the time he left, there had been a scandalous homicide and several trials: the wealthy Jim Williams was accused of killing his assistant and sometime lover, Danny Hansford.

Before you set out, find a copy of the book, pour yourself a cool drink, and enter an eccentric world of cutthroat killers and society backstabbers, voodoo witches, and garden-club ladies. Then head over to the Historic District to follow the characters' steps. By the end of this walking tour, you'll be hard-pressed to find the line between Berendt's creative nonfiction and Savannah's reality. Note: unless otherwise indicated, the sights on this tour are not open to the public.

A Good Walk

Begin at the southwest corner of Monterey Square, site of the **MERCER HOUSE** ㉒, whose construction was begun by songwriter Johnny Mercer's great-grandfather just before the Civil War. Two blocks south on Bull Street is the **ARMSTRONG HOUSE** ㉓, an earlier residence of Jim Williams, the main character in the book. Walk south through Forsyth Park to the corner of Park Avenue and Whitaker Street. The **FORSYTH PARK APARTMENTS** ㉔, where author John Berendt lived, are on the southwest corner of Forsyth Park. Then turn back north through the park. At the midpoint of the park's northern edge, turn north up Bull Street in the direction of Monterey Square. Turn left on West Gordon Street off Bull Street and walk toward the corner of

West Gordon Street and Whitaker Street, where you'll reach **SERENA DAWES'S HOUSE** ㉕. Next, cross West Gordon Street, walk north on Bull Street in front of Mercer House, cross Wayne Street, and you'll find that the first house on the left facing Bull Street at Wayne Street is **LEE ADLER'S HOME** ㉖, which sits across from Monterey Square's northwest corner. Continue walking north on Bull Street and take a right (east) on East Jones Street. **JOE ODOM'S FIRST HOUSE** ㉗ is the third house on the left before Drayton Street.

Continue on East Jones Street to Abercorn Street and turn left (north), walking two blocks on Abercorn Street to East Charlton Street and the **HAMILTON-TURNER HOUSE** ㉘, now a B&B inn. Then swing around Lafayette Square to East Harris Street, and take it about six blocks west to Pulaski Square at Barnard Street; turn right (north) on Barnard Street through Orleans Square and continue north to Telfair Square. On foot, you may elect to head west down West York Street to find the **CHATHAM COUNTY COURTHOUSE** ㉙, scene of all those trials, two blocks away. Finally, take either Whitaker Street or Abercorn Street south to Victory Drive and turn left. Go through Thunderbolt to Whatley Avenue, and turn left again. Whatley Avenue leads directly to Bonaventure Road, which curves in both directions; bear left, and on your right about a quarter mile up the road is **BONAVENTURE CEMETERY** ㉚.

TIMING
Allow a leisurely two hours to walk the main points of the tour, plus another hour to visit the cemetery.

What to See

❷❸ **ARMSTRONG HOUSE.** Antiques dealer Jim Williams lived and worked in this residence before purchasing the Mercer House. On a late-afternoon walk past the mansion, Berendt met Mr. Simon Glover, an 86-year-old singer and porter for the law firm of Bouhan, Williams, and Levy, occupants of the building. Glover confided that he earned a weekly $10 for walking the deceased dogs of a former partner of the firm up and down Bull Street. Baffled? So was the author. Behind the house's cast-iron gates are the offices of Frank Siler, Jim Williams's attorney, who doubles as keeper of Uga, the Georgia Bulldog mascot. *447 Bull St., Historic District.*

30 BONAVENTURE CEMETERY. A cemetery east of downtown is the final resting place for Danny Hansford. The haunting female tombstone figure from the book's cover has been removed to protect surrounding graves from sightseers. Now you can view the figure at the Telfair Mansion. *330 Bonaventure Rd., Eastside, tel. 912/651–6843.*

29 CHATHAM COUNTY COURTHOUSE. The courthouse was the scene of three of Williams's murder trials, which took place over the course of about eight years. An underground tunnel leads from the courthouse to the jail where Williams was held in a cell that was modified to allow him to conduct his antiques business. *133 Montgomery St., Historic District.*

24 FORSYTH PARK APARTMENTS. Here was Berendt's second home in Savannah; from his fourth-floor rooms he pieced together the majority of the book. While parking his newly acquired 1973 Pontiac Grand Prix outside these apartments, Berendt met the Lady Chablis coming out of her nearby doctor's office, freshly feminine from a new round of hormone shots. *Whitaker and Gwinnett Sts., Historic District.*

28 HAMILTON-TURNER HOUSE. After one too many of Joe Odom's deals went sour, Mandy Nichols, his fourth fiancée-in-waiting, left him and took over his third residence, a Second Empire–style mansion dating from 1873. Mandy filled it with 17th- and 18th-century antiques and transformed it into a successful museum through which she led tour groups. The elegant towering hulk is at the southeast corner of Lafayette Square. The house was sold in the late '90s and has since become the elegant Hamilton-Turner Inn. *330 Abercorn St., Historic District.*

㉗ JOE ODOM'S FIRST HOUSE. At this stucco town house, Odom, a combination tax lawyer, real-estate broker, and piano player, hosted a 24-hour stream of visitors. The author met Odom through Mandy Nichols, a former Miss Big Beautiful Woman, who stopped by to borrow ice one time after the power had been cut off, a frequent occurrence. *16 E. Jones St., Historic District.*

㉖ LEE ADLER'S HOME. Just north of the Mercer House, in half of the double town house facing West Wayne Street, Lee Adler, the adversary of Jim Williams, runs his business of restoring historic Savannah properties. Adler's howling dogs drove Williams to his pipe organ, where he churned out a deafening version of César Franck's *Pièce Heroïque.* Later, Adler stuck reelection signs in his front lawn, showing his support for the district attorney who prosecuted Williams three times before he was finally found not guilty. *425 Bull St., Historic District.*

㉒ MERCER HOUSE. This redbrick Italianate mansion on the southwest corner of Monterey Square became Jim Williams's Taj Mahal; here he ran a world-class antiques dealership and held *the* Christmas party of the season; here also Danny Hansford, his sometime house partner, succumbed to gunshot wounds. Williams himself died here of a heart attack in 1990, near the very spot where Hansford fell. Today his sister lives quietly among the remnants of his Fabergé collection and his Joshua Reynolds paintings, in rooms lighted by Waterford crystal chandeliers. *429 Bull St., Historic District.*

㉕ SERENA DAWES'S HOUSE. Near the intersection of West Gordon and Bull streets, this house was owned by Helen Driscoll, also known as Serena Dawes. A high-profile beauty in the 1930s and 1940s, she married into a Pennsylvania steel family. After her husband accidentally and fatally shot himself in the head, she retired here, in her hometown. Dawes, Berendt writes, "spent most of her day in bed, holding court, drinking martinis and pink ladies, playing with her white toy poodle, Lulu." Chief among Serena's gentlemen callers was Luther Driggers, rumored to possess a poison strong enough to wipe out the entire city. *17 W. Gordon St., Historic District.*

OTHER AREA ATTRACTIONS

EBENEZER. When the Salzburgers arrived in Savannah in 1734, Oglethorpe sent them up the Savannah River to establish a settlement. The first effort was assailed by disease, and they sought his permission to move to better ground. Denied, they moved anyway and established Ebenezer. Here, they engaged in silkworm production and, in 1769, built the Jerusalem Church, which still stands. After the revolution, the silkworm operation never resumed, and the town faded into history. Descendants of these Protestant religious refugees have preserved the church and assembled a few of the remaining buildings, moving them to this site from other locations. Be sure to follow Route 275 to its end and see Ebenezer Landing, where the Salzburgers came ashore. *Ebenezer Rd., Rte. 21–Rte. 275, Rincon (25 mi north of Savannah).*

OLD FORT JACKSON. About 2 mi east of Broad Street via President Street, you'll see a sign for the fort, which is 3 mi from the city. Purchased in 1808 by the federal government, this is the oldest standing fort in Georgia. It was garrisoned in 1812 and was the Confederate headquarters of the river batteries. The brick edifice is surrounded by a tidal moat, and there are 13 exhibit areas. Battle reenactments, blacksmithing demonstrations, and programs of 19th-century music are among the fort's activities for tour groups. *1 Ft. Jackson Rd., Fort Jackson, tel. 912/232–3945, www.chsgeorgia.org/fortjackson.cfm. $3.50. Daily 9–5.*

★ ⑮ **FORT PULASKI NATIONAL MONUMENT.** Named for Casimir Pulaski, a Polish count and Revolutionary War hero, this must-see sight for Civil War buffs was built on Cockspur Island between

1829 and 1847. Robert E. Lee's first assignment after graduating from West Point was as an engineer here. During the Civil War the fort fell, on April 11, 1862, after a mere 30 hours of bombardment by newfangled rifled cannons. The restored fortification, operated by the National Park Service, has moats, drawbridges, massive ramparts, and towering walls. The park has trails and picnic areas. It's 14 mi east of downtown Savannah; you'll see the entrance on your left just before U.S. 80 reaches Tybee Island. *U.S. 80, Fort Pulaski, tel. 912/786–5787, www.nps.gov/fopu. $3. Daily 9–5.*

MELON BLUFF. On a centuries-old 3,000-acre plantation that has been in one family since 1735, Melon Bluff includes a nature center and facilities for canoeing, kayaking, bird-watching, hiking, and other outdoor activities. You can camp here or stay at one of the three B&B inns ($$–$$$): Palmyra Plantation, an 1850s cottage; the Ripley Farmhouse, a classic rural house with a tin-covered roof; and an old barn, renovated to contain nine guest rooms. From Melon Bluff you can visit nearby **Seabrook Village,** a small but growing cluster of rural buildings from an African-American historic community; **Old Sunbury,** whose port made it a viable competitor to Savannah until the Revolutionary War ended its heyday; **Fort Morris,** which protected Savannah during the revolution; and **Midway,** an 18th-century village with a house museum and period cemetery. To reach Melon Bluff, take I–95 south from Savannah (about 30 mi) to Exit 76 (Midway/Sunbury), turn left, and go east for 3 mi. The other sites mentioned here are all within a short drive. *2999 Islands Hwy., Midway, tel. 912/884–5779 or 888/246–8188, fax 912/884–3046, www.melonbluff.com.*

MIGHTY EIGHTH AIR FORCE HERITAGE MUSEUM. The famous World War II squadron the Mighty Eighth Air Force was formed in Savannah in January 1942 and shipped out to the United Kingdom. Flying Royal Air Force aircraft, the Mighty Eighth became the largest air force of the period, with some 200,000 combat crew personnel. Many lost their lives during raids on enemy factories or were interned as prisoners of war. Exhibits begin with the prelude to World War II and the rise of Adolf Hitler and continue through Desert Storm. *175 Bourne Ave. (I–95, Exit 102, to U.S. 80), Pooler (14 mi west of Savannah), tel. 912/748–8888, www.mightyeighth.org. $8. Daily 9–5.*

SKIDAWAY MARINE SCIENCE COMPLEX. On the grounds of the former Modena Plantation, Skidaway has a 14-panel, 12,000-gallon aquarium with marine and plant life of the continental shelf. Other exhibits highlight coastal archaeology and fossils of the Georgia coast. Nature trails overlook marsh and water. *30 Ocean Science Circle, Skidaway Island (8 mi south of Savannah), tel. 912/598–2496. $2. Weekdays 9–4, Sat. noon–5.*

TYBEE ISLAND. *Tybee* is an Indian word meaning "salt." The Yamacraw Indians came to this island in the Atlantic Ocean to hunt and fish, and legend has it that pirates buried their treasure here. The island is about 5 mi long and 2 mi wide, with seafood restaurants, chain motels, condos, and shops—most of which sprang up during the 1950s and haven't changed much since. The entire expanse of white sand is divided into a number of public beaches, where you can shell and crab, charter fishing boats, and swim. It's 18 mi east of Savannah; take Victory Drive (U.S. 80), sometimes called Tybee Road, onto the island. On your way here stop by Fort Jackson and Fort Pulaski National Monument. Nearby, the misnamed Little Tybee Island, actually larger than Tybee Island, is entirely undeveloped. Contact **Tybee Island Convention and Visitors Bureau** (*Box 491, Tybee Island 31328, tel. 800/868–2322, www.tybeevisit.com*).

EATING OUT

Savannah has excellent seafood restaurants, though locals also have a passion for spicy barbecued meats. The Historic District yields culinary treasures, especially along River Street. Several of the city's restaurants—such as Elizabeth on 37th, 45 South, the

Olde Pink House, and Sapphire Grill—have been beacons that have drawn members of the culinary upper crust to the region for decades. From there they explored and discovered that such divine dining isn't isolated to Savannah's Historic District, as nearby Thunderbolt, Skidaway, Tybee, and Wilmington islands also have a collection of remarkable restaurants.

CATEGORY	COST*
$$$$	over $30
$$$	$20–$30
$$	$10–$20
$	under $10

*per person for a main course at dinner

$$$–$$$$ **ELIZABETH ON 37TH.** Regional specialties are the hallmark at this
★ acclaimed restaurant that goes so far as to credit local produce suppliers on its menu. Chef Elizabeth Terry manages to make dishes such as Maryland crab cakes and a plate of roasted shiitake and oyster mushrooms sit comfortably beside Southern-fried grits and country ham. The extravagant Savannah cream cake is the way to finish your meal in this elegant turn-of-the-20th-century mansion with hardwood floors and spacious rooms. 105 E. 37th St., Victorian District, tel. 912/236–5547. Reservations essential. AE, D, DC, MC, V. No lunch.

$$$–$$$$ **45 SOUTH.** This popular Southside eatery is small and stylish, with
★ a contemporary mauve-and-green interior. The game-heavy menu often includes a confit of tender rabbit with morels and mashed potatoes. 20 E. Broad St., Victorian District, tel. 912/233–1881. Reservations essential. AE, D, DC, MC, V. Closed Sun. No lunch.

$$–$$$ **BELFORD'S STEAK AND SEAFOOD.** In the heart of City Market, Belford's is great for Sunday brunch, when so many of the downtown venues are closed. A complimentary glass of sparkling wine arrives at your table when you place your order. Brunch entrées include egg dishes, such as smoked salmon Florentine and crab frittatas. The lunch and dinner menus focus on seafood, including Georgia

savannah dining and lodging

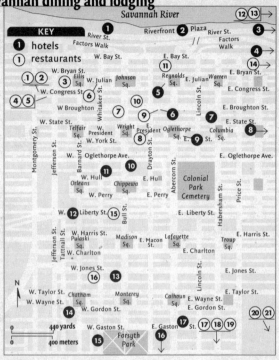

Savannah River

KEY

1 hotels

1 restaurants

Dining

Belford's Steak and Seafood, **3**

Bistro Savannah, **5**

Cafe@Main, **7**

Creole Red, **2**

Elizabeth on 37th, **20**

45 South, **14**

George's of Tybee, **13**

Il Pasticcio, **10**

Johnny Harris, **21**

The Lady & Sons, **4**

Mrs. Wilkes Dining Room, **16**

Nita's Place, **9**

North Beach Grill, **12**

Olde Pink House, **11**

Red, Hot & Blue, **17**

Sapphire Grill, **6**

Savannah Steak House, **1**

17 Hundred and 90, **8**

SoHo South Cafe, **15**

Toucan Cafe, **18**

Yanni's Greek Cuisine, **19**

Lodging

Ballastone Inn, **10**

Bed & Breakfast Inn, **14**

Claudia's Manor, **16**

Eliza Thompson House, **13**

Foley House Inn, **11**

Gastonian, **17**

Green Palm Inn, **8**

Hyatt Regency Savannah, **1**

Kehoe House, **7**

Magnolia Place Inn, **15**

The Manor House, **12**

Marshall House, **6**

Mulberry Inn, **4**

Planters Inn, **5**

The President's Quarters, **9**

River Street Inn, **2**.

17th Street Inn, **3**

pecan grouper and Lowcountry shrimp and grits. 315 W. St. Julian St., Historic District, tel. 912/233–2626. AE, D, DC, MC, V.

$$–$$$ **BISTRO SAVANNAH.** High ceilings, burnished heart-pine floors, ★ and gray-brick walls lined with local art contribute to the bistroish qualities of this spot by City Market. The menu has such specialties as seared beef tenderloin with shiitakes, scallions, corn pancakes and horseradish sauce, and shrimp and tasso (seasoned cured pork) on stone-ground grits. Another treat is the crispy roasted duck. 309 W. Congress St., Historic District, tel. 912/233–6266. AE, MC, V. No lunch.

$$–$$$ **CAFE@MAIN.** This upscale but easygoing restaurant offers a compendium of Continental and regional American dishes, such as pork tenderloin with mashed potatoes and fresh green beans, and potato-onion-crusted grouper. Also of note is the wine list, with an unusually extensive selection of by-the-glass offerings. 1 W. Broughton St., Historic District, tel. 912/447–5979. AE, MC, V.

$$–$$$ **GEORGES' OF TYBEE.** From the proprietors of the North Beach Grill came Tybee's first fine restaurant. The warmly lighted interior, with its inviting dining room, with a lovely stone fireplace and dark rose-painted walls, is a fine place to spend a romantic evening. Duck liver and frisée salad, and Thai-barbecued Muscovy duck breast are popular. Lobster, crab, and four-cheese ravioli with carrots, snow peas, and arugula, in a saffron-cream sauce, is also outstanding. 1105 E. U.S. 80, Tybee Island, tel. 912/786–9730. AE, MC, V. Closed Mon. No lunch.

$$–$$$ **IL PASTICCIO.** Sicilian Pino Venetico turned this former department ★ store into his dream restaurant—a bistro-style place gleaming with steel, glass, and tile, and a lively, hip, young crowd to populate it. The menu changes frequently, but fresh pastas and sauces are a constant. Don't miss the second-floor art gallery. Excellent desserts, including a superior tiramisu, make this one worth seeking out. 2 E. Broughton St., Historic District, tel. 912/231–8888. AE, D, DC, MC, V. No lunch.

$$–$$$ OLDE PINK HOUSE. The brick Georgian mansion was built in 1771 for James Habersham, one of the wealthiest Americans of his time. One of Savannah's oldest buildings, the tavern has original Georgia pine floors, Venetian chandeliers, and 18th-century English antiques. The she-crab soup is a light but flavorful version of this Lowcountry specialty. Regional ingredients find their way into many of the dishes, including the black grouper stuffed with blue crab and served with a Vidalia onion sauce. *23 Abercorn St., Historic District, tel. 912/232–4286. AE, MC, V. No lunch.*

$$–$$$ SAPPHIRE GRILL. Savannah's young and restless pack this trendy
★ haunt nightly. Chef Chris Nason focuses his seasonal menus on local ingredients, such as Georgia white shrimp, crab, and fish. Vegetarians will delight in his elegant vegetable presentations—perhaps including roasted sweet onions, spicy peppers, wild mushrooms, or roasted shallots. Chocoholics: get the remarkably delicious, intensely potent chocolate flan. *110 W. Congress St., Historic District, tel. 912/443–9962. Reservations essential. AE, D, DC, MC, V. No lunch.*

$$–$$$ SAVANNAH STEAK HOUSE. This art-filled, dashing restaurant with a striking collage on its ceiling has made an impressive splash in Savannah dining circles. The menu offers a tremendously varied number of inventive delicacies. Traditionalists might stick with the hefty rib-eye steak, but if you're game for something more exotic, consider "wild" entrées such as ostrich fillet, wild-boar chili, and antelope medallions. *423 W. Congress St., Historic District, tel. 912/232–0092. AE, MC, V. Closed Sun.*

$$–$$$ 17 HUNDRED AND 90. Chef Deborah Noelk keeps a creative
★ kitchen in this restaurant—in a rustic structure dating to the 13th colony and tucked in among ancient oaks dripping with Spanish moss. The restaurant is in Savannah's oldest inn of the same name. Entrées include pan-seared veal medallions with artichoke hearts and capers in a lemon butter; roasted half duckling with a port wine lingonberry sauce; and local shrimp stuffed with scallops and crabmeat and served with a lemon beurre blanc

sauce. There is a ghost story to go with dinner, so make sure the waiter fills you in. *307 E. Presidents St., Historic District, tel. 912/231–8888. AE, D, DC, MC, V. No lunch weekends.*

$$–$$$ **THE LADY & SONS.** Expect to take your place in line, along with locals, here. Everyone patiently waits to attack the buffet, which is stocked for both lunch and dinner with such specials as moist, crispy fried chicken; the best baked spaghetti in the South; green beans cooked with ham and potatoes; tender, sweet creamed corn; and homemade lemonade. The interior of this 1870s-era building, painted pale pink with faux ivy tendrils draped along its perimeter, is bright, cheerful, and busy. Owner Paula H. Deen's book, *The Lady & Sons: Savannah Country Cookbook,* includes recipes for the most popular dishes. *311 W. Congress St., Historic District, tel. 912/233–2600. AE, D, MC, V. No dinner Sun.*

$$ **JOHNNY HARRIS.** What started as a small roadside stand in 1924 has grown into one of the city's mainstays, with a menu that includes steaks, fried chicken, seafood, and meats spiced with the restaurant's famous tomato-and-mustard sauce. The lamb barbecue is a treat, and their sauces are now so famous that they bottle them for take-home and shipping. There's live music Friday and Saturday nights, except on the first Saturday night of the month, when there's dancing. *1651 E. Victory Dr., Eastside, tel. 912/354–7810. AE, D, DC, MC, V. Closed Sun.*

$$ ★ **MRS. WILKES DINING ROOM.** Folks line up for a culinary orgy of fine Southern food, served family style at big tables. For breakfast there are eggs, sausage, piping hot biscuits, and grits. At lunch try fried or roast chicken, collard greens, okra, mashed potatoes, and corn bread. *107 W. Jones St., Historic District, tel. 912/232–5997. Reservations not accepted. No credit cards. Closed Jan. and weekends. No dinner.*

$$ **NORTH BEACH GRILL.** The tiny kitchen of this casual beachfront locale serves up a taste of the Caribbean. The jerk-rubbed fish tacos with fruit salsa—which you'll be hard-pressed to find prepared right in the South—are wonderful. Also expect to be tempted by the grilled okra and by the sea bass topped with caramelized onions with cilantro-lime beurre blanc. You can come in a swimsuit for lunch, but throw on something casual for dinner. *41A Meddin Dr., Tybee Island, tel. 912/786–9003. Reservations not accepted. D, MC, V. Closed weekdays Dec.–Jan.*

$-$$ **NITA'S PLACE.** Juanita Dixon has a reputation for perfectly
★ preparing down-home Southern cooking at this renowned steam-table operation, which remains authentic (despite now being housed in a more polished-looking space than its original location). People flock here for salmon patties, baked chicken, perfectly cooked okra, outstanding squash casserole, and homemade desserts. The fresh vegetables and other side dishes alone are worth the trip, if only for the sheer number (11) from which to choose: rutabagas, fried corn, string beans, potato salad, collard greens, sautéed spinach, black-eyed peas, macaroni and cheese, fried sweet potatoes, baked sweet potatoes, and Nita's famous squash casserole. *129 E. Broughton St., Historic District, tel. 912/238–8233. Reservations not accepted. MC, V. Closed Sun. No dinner Mon.–Thurs.*

$-$$ **RED HOT & BLUE.** Their motto is: "Best Barbecue You'll Ever
★ Have in a Building that Hasn't Already Been Condemned!" With such specialties as pulled-pig spare ribs, pork spare ribs, beef brisket, smoked chicken, and smoked sausage, all meticulously smoked over hickory wood for a long time, this place may be worth the drive to the Southside for barbecue aficionados, even if it is a chain location. *11108 Abercorn St., Southside, tel. 912/961–7422. Reservations not accepted. MC, V.*

$-$$ **SOHO SOUTH CAFE.** This is not your normal soup-and-salad pit stop—it's a soup-and-salad pit stop for epicureans. The tuna salad in your tuna-salad sandwich will be made to order—from the café's own recipe, no less—and the smoked ham and Brie on a baguette is enough to make your taste buds swoon. The soups are also fittingly fabulous. 12 W. Liberty St., Historic District, tel. 912/233–1633. MC, V. Closed Sun. Dinner served 6–9:30 Fri.–Sat. only.

$–$$ TOUCAN CAFE. This colorful café has food to satisfy every kind of eater—the menu is sympathetic to vegetarian tastes but doesn't leave meat eaters out in the cold. Offerings include Indian veggie *samosas* with curried broccoli, Jamaican jerk chicken, and rib-eye steaks. 531 Stephenson Ave., Southside, tel. 912/352–2233. AE, D, MC, V. Closed Sun.

$–$$ YANNI'S GREEK CUISINE. A gregarious waitstaff serves a wonderful,
★ authentic Greek cuisine in this Southside eatery with walls emblazoned by murals of Mediterranean seaside panoramas. Menu items include Grecian shrimp kebabs with feta, garlic, onions and tomatoes, as well as salmon sautéed in a creamy white-wine and dill sauce. There is plenty of pork, beef, and chicken to choose from as well, all prepared with finesse. 11211 Abercorn Expressway, Southside, tel. 912/925–6814. AE, D, MC, V. Closed Sun.

$ CREOLE RED. This jaunty little no-frills storefront café is patronized with great enthusiasm by locals. Everybody seems to love the delicious and inexpensive Louisiana specialties, from fresh crawfish étouffée to deviled crabs, served with warmth and aplomb by the friendly proprietor and staff. 409 W. Congress St., Historic District, tel. 912/234–6690. MC, V.

SHOPPING

Find your own Lowcountry treasures among a bevy of handcrafted wares—handmade quilts and baskets; wreaths made from Chinese tallow trees and Spanish moss; preserves, jams, and jellies. The favorite Savannah snack, and a popular gift item, is the benne wafer. It's about the size of a quarter and comes in different flavors. Savannah has a wide collection of colorful businesses—revitalization is no longer a goal but an accomplishment. Antiques malls and junk emporiums beckon you with their colorful storefronts and eclectic offerings, as do the many specialty shops and bookstores clustered along the moss-embossed streets.

SHOPPING DISTRICTS

CITY MARKET (W. St. Julian St. between Ellis and Franklin Sqs., Historic District) has sidewalk cafés, jazz haunts, shops, and art galleries. **RIVERFRONT PLAZA/RIVER STREET** (Historic District) is nine blocks of shops in renovated waterfront warehouses where you can find everything from popcorn to pottery.

SPECIALTY SHOPS

Antiques

ALEXANDRA'S ANTIQUE GALLERY (320 W. Broughton St., Historic District, tel. 912/233–3999) is a four-level extravaganza of items from kitsch to fine antiques. **ARTHUR SMITH ANTIQUES** (402 Bull St., Historic District, tel. 912/236–9701) has four floors showcasing 18th- and 19th-century European furniture, porcelain, rugs, and paintings.

Art Galleries

COMPASS PRINTS, INC./RAY ELLIS GALLERY (205 W. Congress St., Historic District, tel. 912/234–3537) sells original artwork, prints, and books by internationally acclaimed artist Ray Ellis. **GALLERY ESPRESSO** (6 E. Liberty St., Historic District, tel. 912/233–5348) has a new show every two weeks focusing on work by local artists. A true coffeehouse, it stays open until the wee hours. **GALLERY 209** (209 E. River St., Historic District, tel. 912/236–4583) is a co-op gallery, with paintings, watercolors, pottery, jewelry, batik, stained glass, weavings, and sculptures by local artists. **JACK LEIGH GALLERY** (132 E. Oglethorpe Ave., Historic District, tel. 912/234–6449) displays the work of Jack Leigh, whose photograph of Bonaventure Cemetery graces the cover of *Midnight in the Garden of Good and Evil*. **OFF THE WALL** (206 W. Broughton St., Historic District, tel. 912/233–8840) exhibits artists from everywhere, including Savannah.

SAVANNAH COLLEGE OF ART AND DESIGN (516 Abercorn St., Historic District, tel. 912/525–5200), a private art college, has restored at least 40 historic buildings in the city, including 12 galleries. Work by faculty and students is often for sale, and touring exhibitions are frequently in the on-campus galleries. Stop by Exhibit A, Pinnacle Gallery, and the West Bank Gallery, and ask about other student galleries. Garden for the Arts has an amphitheater and shows performance art.

Benne Wafers

BYRD COOKIE COMPANY & GOURMET MARKETPLACE (6700 Waters Ave., Highland Park, tel. 912/355–1716), founded in 1924, is the best place to get the popular cookies that are also sold in numerous gift shops around town.

Books

For regional to general Southern subjects and Americana, visit the **BOOK LADY** (17 W. York St., Historic District, tel. 912/233–3628), in a 200-year-old house for more than two decades. The shop also has an online search service. **E. SHAVER BOOKSELLERS** (326 Bull St., Historic District, tel. 912/234–7257) is the source for 17th- and 18th-century maps and new books on regional subjects; the shop occupies 12 rooms. **V. & J. DUNCAN** (12 E. Taylor St., Historic District, tel. 912/232–0338) specializes in antique maps, prints, and books.

Country Crafts

CHARLOTTE'S CORNER (1 W. Liberty St., Historic District, tel. 912/233–8061) carries expensive and moderately priced Savannah souvenirs, children's clothes and toys, and beachwear.

OUTDOOR ACTIVITIES AND SPORTS

BOATING

At the **BULL RIVER YACHT CLUB MARINA** (8005 Old Tybee Rd., Tybee Island, tel. 912/897–7300), you can arrange a dolphin tour, a deep-sea fishing expedition, or a jaunt through the coastal islands. **LAKE MAYER PARK** (Montgomery Crossroads Rd. and Sallie Mood Dr., Cresthill, tel. 912/652–6780) has paddleboats, sailing, canoeing, and an in-line skating and hockey facility. **SALTWATER CHARTERS** (111 Wickersham Dr., Skidaway Island, tel. 912/598–1814) provides packages ranging from two-hour sightseeing tours to 13-hour deep-sea fishing expeditions. Water taxis to the coastal islands are also available. Public boat ramps are found at **BELL'S ON THE RIVER** (12500 Apache Ave., off Abercorn St., Windward, tel. 912/920–1113), on the Forest River. **SAVANNAH ISLANDS EXPRESSWAY** (adjacent to Frank W. Spencer Park, Skidaway Island, tel. 912/231–8222) offers boat ramps on the Wilmington River. **SAVANNAH MARINA** (Thunderbolt, tel. 912/897–3625) provides ramps on the Wilmington River.

GOLF

BACON PARK (1 Shorty Cooper Dr., Southside, tel. 912/354–2625), a public course with 27 holes, is par 72 for 18 holes and has a lighted driving range. **HENDERSON GOLF CLUB** (1 Al Henderson Dr., at I–95, Exit 94 to Rte. 204, Southside, tel. 912/920–4653) is an 18-hole, par-71 course about 15 mi from downtown Savannah. The **MARY CALDER GOLF COURSE** (W. Lathrop Ave., West Chatham, tel. 912/238–7100) is par 35 for its 9 holes.

JOGGING AND RUNNING

Savannah's low-lying coastal terrain makes it an ideal place for joggers. **FORSYTH PARK** (Bull St. between Whitaker and

Drayton Sts., Historic District) is a flat, pleasant place to walk, jog, or run. **TYBEE ISLAND** has a white-sand beach that is hard packed and relatively debris free, making it a favorite with runners. For suburban jogging trails head for **DAFFIN PARK** (1500 E. Victory Dr., Edgemere), with level sidewalks available during daylight hours. **LAKE MAYER PARK** (Montgomery Crossroads Rd. and Sallie Mood Dr., Southside) has 1½ mi of level asphalt available 24 hours a day.

TENNIS

BACON PARK (6262 Skidaway Rd., Southside, tel. 912/351–3850) has 16 lighted asphalt courts. Fees are $2.50 an hour per person. **FORSYTH PARK** (Drayton St. and Park Ave., Historic District, tel. 912/652–6780) contains four lighted courts available until about 10 PM; there is no charge to use them. **LAKE MAYER PARK** (Montgomery Crossroads Rd. and Sallie Mood Dr., Southside, tel. 912/652–6780) has eight asphalt lighted courts available at no charge and open 8 AM–10 PM (until 11 PM May–September).

NIGHTLIFE AND THE ARTS

Savannah's nightlife reflects the city's laid-back personality. Some clubs have live reggae, hard rock, and other contemporary music, but most stick to traditional blues, jazz, and piano-bar vocalists. After-dark merrymakers usually head for watering holes on Riverfront Plaza or the south side.

BARS AND NIGHTCLUBS

The **BAR BAR** (219 W. St. Julian St., Historic District, tel. 912/231–1910), a neighborhood hangout, has pool tables, games, and a varied beer selection. Once a month at **CLUB ONE JEFFERSON** (1 Jefferson St., Historic District, tel. 912/232–0200), a gay bar, the Lady Chablis bumps and grinds her way down the catwalk, lip-synching disco tunes in a shimmer of sequin and satin gowns; the cover is $5. **KEVIN BARRY'S IRISH PUB** (114 W. River St., Historic District, tel. 912/233–9626) has a friendly vibe, a full menu until 1 AM, and traditional Irish music from Wednesday to Sunday; it's the place to be on St. Patrick's Day. The rest of the year there's a mix of tourists and locals of all ages. Go to **M.D.'S LOUNGE** (2 W. Bay St., Historic District, tel. 912/238–1234) if you have a classy nightcap in mind. The bar is literally perched above the Savannah River and surrounded by windows big enough to be glass walls. **STOGIES** (112 W. Congress St., Historic District, tel. 912/233–4277) has its own humidor where patrons buy expensive cigars. It's a fun spot if you can take the smoke.

COFFEEHOUSES

Thanks to a substantial student population, the city has sprouted coffeehouses as if they were spring flowers. **CHRISTY'S ESPRESSO DELIGHTS** (7400 Abercorn St., Highland Park, tel. 912/356–3566) is a full-service espresso café with a wonderful selection of fine desserts and a light-lunch menu. The **EXPRESS** (39 Barnard St., Historic District, tel. 912/233–4683) is a warm, unassuming bakery and café that serves specialty coffees along with decadent desserts and tasty snacks. **GALLERY ESPRESSO** (6 E. Liberty St., Historic District, tel. 912/233–5348) is a combined coffee haunt and art enclave, with gallery shows; it stays open late.

JAZZ AND BLUES CLUBS

BAYOU CAFÉ AND BLUES BAR (14 N. Abercorn St., at River St., Historic District, tel. 912/233–6414) has acoustic music during the week and the Bayou Blues Band on the weekend. The food is Cajun. **CAFE LOCO** (1 Old Hwy. 80, Tybee Island, tel. 912/786–7810), a few miles outside Savannah, showcases local blues and acoustic acts. You can rollick with Emma Kelly, the undisputed "Lady of 6,000 Songs," at **HARD HEARTED HANNAH'S EAST** (20 E. Broad St., Historic District, tel. 912/233–2225) Tuesday through Saturday.

WHERE TO STAY

Although Savannah has its share of chain hotels and motels, the city's most distinctive lodgings are the more than two dozen historic inns, guest houses, and B&Bs gracing the Historic District.

If the term *historic inn* brings to mind images of roughing it in shabby-genteel mansions with antiquated plumbing, you're in for a surprise. Most of these inns are in mansions with the requisite high ceilings, spacious rooms, and ornate carved millwork. And most do have canopy, four-poster, or Victorian brass beds. But amid all the antique surroundings, there is modern luxury: enormous baths, many with whirlpools or hot tubs; film libraries for in-room VCRs; and turndown service with a chocolate, a praline, even a discreet brandy on your nightstand. Continental breakfast and afternoon refreshments are often included in the rate. Prices have risen since the filming of *Midnight in the Garden of Good and Evil*. Special seasons and holidays, such as St. Patrick's Day, push prices up a bit as well. On the other hand, weekdays and the off-season can yield excellent bargains.

CATEGORY	SAVANNAH*
$$$$	over $230
$$$	$170–$230
$$	$100–$170
$	under $100

*All prices are for a standard double room, excluding 13% tax and service.

INNS AND GUEST HOUSES

$$$$ **GASTONIAN.** Guest rooms at this inn, built in 1868, have working
★ fireplaces and antiques from the Georgian and Regency periods; most also have whirlpool tubs or Japanese soak tubs. The Caracalla Suite is named for the oversize whirlpool tub built in front of the

fireplace. At breakfast you'll find such specialty items as ginger pancakes. Afternoon tea, evening cordials, and complimentary wine are other treats. *220 E. Gaston St., Historic District, 31401, tel. 912/232–2869 or 800/322–6603, fax 912/232–0710, www. gastonian.com. 14 rooms, 3 suites. Internet. AE, D, MC, V. BP.*

$$$–$$$$ **BALLASTONE INN.** This sumptuous inn occupies an 1838 mansion
★ that once served as a bordello. Rooms are handsomely furnished, with luxurious linens on canopy beds, antiques and fine reproductions, and a collection of original framed prints from *Harper's* scattered throughout. On the garden level rooms are small and cozy, with exposed brick walls, beam ceilings, and, in some cases, windows at eye level with the lush courtyard. Most rooms have working gas fireplaces, and three have whirlpool tubs. Afternoon tea and free passes to a nearby health club are included. *14 E. Oglethorpe Ave., Historic District, 31401, tel. 912/236–1484 or 800/822–4553, fax 912/236–4626, www.ballastone.com. 14 rooms, 3 suites. In-room VCRs, bicycles. AE, MC, V. BP.*

$$$–$$$$ **ELIZA THOMPSON HOUSE.** Eliza Thompson was a socially prominent widow when she built her fine town house around 1847; today the lovely Victorian edifice remains one of the oldest B&Bs in Savannah. The lovingly weathered exterior still retains the majestic beauty of its stately heyday, when regal homes were all the rage. A peaceful garden courtyard provides a quiet respite where you can read or simply breathe in the floral scents. The rooms are lavishly decorated, with marble baths and rare antiques, boasting walls painted in deep primaries, such as forest green or pencil yellow—which provide stunning backdrops for the plush bedding and other designer accents. Continental breakfast and complimentary afternoon wine and cheese are served in the parlor or on the patio, with its fine Ivan Bailey sculpture. *5 W. Jones St., Historic District, 31401, tel. 912/236–3620 or 800/348–9378, fax 912/238–1920, www.elizathompsonhouse.com. 25 rooms. MC, V. BP.*

$$$–$$$$ **FOLEY HOUSE INN.** Two town houses, built 50 years apart, form
★ this elegant inn. Proprietor Phillip Jenkins often entertains during

the evening wine-and-dessert service—he plays lively numbers on the baby grand piano in the parlor. Most rooms have antiques and reproductions; five rooms have whirlpool tubs. A carriage house to the rear of the property has less expensive rooms. *14 W. Hull St., Historic District, 31401, tel. 912/232–6622 or 800/647–3708, fax 912/231–1218, www.foleyinn.com. 17 rooms, 2 suites. In-room VCRs. AE, MC, V. BP.*

$$$–$$$$ **KEHOE HOUSE.** A fabulously appointed 1890s B&B, the Victorian Kehoe House has brass-and-marble chandeliers, a courtyard garden, and a music room. On the main floor a double parlor holds two fireplaces and sweeps the eye upward with its 14-ft ceilings. Turndown service is included. Rates include access to the Downtown Athletic Club. *123 Habersham St., Historic District, 31401, tel. 912/232–1020 or 800/820–1020, fax 912/231–0208, www.kehoehouse.com. 13 rooms, 2 suites. Meeting room. AE, D, DC, MC, V. BP.*

$$–$$$$ **MAGNOLIA PLACE INN.** Looking out directly across breathtaking
★ Forsyth Park, this opulent 1878 inn dazzles. There are regal antiques, prints, and porcelain from around the world—you'd expect one of Savannah's wealthy old cotton merchants to occupy such a mansion. Many rooms have Jacuzzis and fireplaces. With expansive verandas, lush terraces, and soaring ceilings, the Magnolia Place Inn typifies Savannah's golden era. *503 Whitaker St., Historic District, 31401, tel. 912/236–7674 or 800/238–7674, fax 912/231–1218, www.magnoliaplaceinn.com. 13 rooms, 3 suites, 2 town houses. In-room VCRs, Internet. AE, MC, V. BP.*

$$–$$$ **CLAUDIA'S MANOR.** Proprietors Claudia and Larry Collins create a warm and inviting feeling in this sweeping Spanish Mediterranean home in the southern reaches of the city's Historic District, just a half mile south of Forsyth Park. Some of the accommodations in this turn-of-the-20th-century house have themed decors— one has African furnishings, and another is a homage to the East. Each of the large suites has a pair of queen-size beds. *101 E. 35th St., Historic District, 31401, tel. 912/233–2379 or 800/773–8177, fax*

912/238–5919, www.claudiasmanor.com. 4 rooms, 3 suites. AE, DC, MC, V. Internet, business services, meeting room. BP.

\$\$–\$\$\$ THE MANOR HOUSE. Built for the Lewis Byrd family in the ★ 1830s, this majestic historic structure (it's the city's oldest building south of Liberty Street) once housed Union officers during General Sherman's Civil War march to the sea. All rooms are suites with a master bedroom and a separate cozy sitting area, and each has been decorated with a delightful individuality. Some even come complete with fireplace and kitchen. The Manor House also oversees three additional properties off-site from the main inn: a gorgeous, antiques-filled loft suite on Factors Walk overlooking the historic Savannah waterfront; a large historic town house complete with formal dining room on Broughton Street; and a magnificent, two-bedroom oceanfront town house with two sprawling private decks on Tybee Island. 201 W. Liberty St., Historic District, 31401, tel. 912/233–9597 or 800/ 462–3595, www.manorhouse-savannah.com. 8 suites. In-room VCRs, some whirlpool baths. AE, D, DC, MC, V. BP.

\$\$–\$\$\$ THE PRESIDENT'S QUARTERS. You'll be impressed even before ★ you enter this lovely inn, which has an exterior courtyard so beautiful and inviting it has become a popular wedding-reception spot. Each room in this classic Savannah inn, fashioned out of a pair of meticulously restored 1860s town houses, is named for an American president. Some rooms have four-poster beds, working fireplaces, and private balconies. Expect to be greeted with wine and fruit, and a complimentary afternoon tea will tempt you with sweet cakes. Turndown service includes a glass of port or sherry. There are also rooms in an adjacent town house. 225 E. President St., Historic District, 31401, tel. 912/233–1600 or 800/233–1776, fax 912/238–0849, www.presidentsquarters.com. 11 rooms, 8 suites. Some hot tubs. D, DC, MC, V. BP.

\$–\$\$ BED & BREAKFAST INN. So called, the owner claims, because it was the first such property to open in Savannah more than 20 years ago, the inn is a restored 1853 federal-style row house on historic

Gordon Row near Chatham Square. The courtyard garden is a lovely cluster of potted tropical flowers surrounding an inviting koi pond. A sweeping renovation has added private baths to all the rooms but managed to keep many elements of the original charm, such as beamed ceilings and exposed-brick walls; only the Garden Suite has a full kitchen. Afternoon pastries, lemonade, coffee, and tea are served. *117 W. Gordon St., Historic District, 31401, tel. 912/ 238–0518, fax 912/233–2537, www.savannahbnb.com. 15 rooms. AE, D, MC, V. BP.*

$–$$ **GREEN PALM INN.** This inn is quite a pleasing little discovery.
★ Originally built in 1897 but renovated top to bottom by owners Jack Moore and Rick Ellison, it's now a B&B. The elegant furnishings, meant to reflect a minimized subtropical aesthetic, were inspired by Savannah's British colonial heritage; some rooms have fireplaces. A separate cottage has two bedrooms, a fireplace, and a lush garden with a marble wading pool. *548 E. President St., Historic District, 31401, tel. 912/447–8901 or 888/606–9510, fax 912/ 236–4626, www.greenpalminn.com. 5 suites, 1 cottage. Fans, cable TV. AE, MC, V. BP.*

$–$$ **17TH STREET INN.** The deck of this 1920 inn, which is adorned with plants, palms, and swings, is a gathering place where you can chat, sip wine, and enjoy breakfast both with other guests and your hosts: Susie Morris and her spouse, Stuart Liles. Steps from the beach, the inn has two-story porches and brightly colored rooms, each with a double iron bed. *12 17th St., Box 114, Tybee Island 31328, tel. 912/786–0607 or 888/909–0607, fax 912/786–0601, www.tybeeinn.com. 8 rooms, 1 condo. Kitchenettes. D, MC, V. CP.*

HOTELS AND MOTELS

$$$–$$$$ **HYATT REGENCY SAVANNAH.** When this riverfront hotel was built in 1981, preservationists opposed the construction of the seven-story modern structure in the Historic District. The main architectural features are the towering atrium and glass elevators. Rooms have modern furnishings, marble baths, and balconies

overlooking either the atrium or the Savannah River. MD's Lounge is the ideal spot to have a drink and watch the river traffic drift by. Windows, the hotel's restaurant, serves a great Sunday buffet. *2 W. Bay St., Historic District, 31401, tel. 912/238–1234 or 800/233–1234, fax 912/944–3673, www.savannah-online.com/hyatt. 325 rooms, 22 suites. Restaurant, bar, indoor pool, health club, lounge, business services, meeting rooms. AE, D, MC, V.*

$$$ MULBERRY INN. ★ This Holiday Inn–managed property is ensconced in an 1860s livery stable that later became a cotton warehouse and then a Coca-Cola bottling plant. Gleaming heart-pine floors and antiques, including a handsome English grandfather clock and an exquisitely carved Victorian mantel, make it unique. Deluxe-grade rooms, as expected, have extras; the 24 suites have living rooms and wet bars. The café is a notch nicer than most other Holiday Inn restaurants. An executive wing, at the back of the hotel, is geared to business travelers. *601 E. Bay St., Historic District, 31401, tel. 912/238–1200 or 800/465–4329, fax 912/236–2184, www.savannahhotel.com. 145 rooms, 24 suites. Restaurant, bar, café, some in-room VCRs, some microwaves, some refrigerators, outdoor pool, outdoor hot tub, Internet, meeting room. AE, D, DC, MC, V.*

$$$ PLANTERS INN. ★ Formerly the John Wesley Hotel, this inn is housed in a structure built in 1812, and though it retains the regal tone of that golden age, it still offers all the intimate comforts you would expect from an upscale inn. The inn's 60 guest rooms are all decorated in the finest fabrics and Baker furnishings (a '20s design style named for the Dutch immigrant cabinetmaker). According to lore, a (good) ghost inhabits the hotel, floating through the hallways and rearranging skewed paintings hanging in the hallway. *29 Abercorn St., Historic District, 31401, tel. 912/232–5678, fax 912/236–2184, www.plantersinnsavannah.com. 60 rooms. Cable TV, hot tubs. AE, D, DC, MC, V.*

$$–$$$ MARSHALL HOUSE. This restored hotel, with original pine floors, woodwork, and bricks, caters to business travelers while providing the intimacy of a B&B. Different spaces reflect different parts of Savannah's history, from its founding to the Civil War. Artwork is mostly by local artists. You can listen to live jazz on weekends in the hotel lounge. Café M specializes in local cuisine, such as Southern pot-au-feu, a seafood-rich Lowcountry dish with okra and greens, and Georgia smoked quail. Guests get free passes to a downtown health club. *123 E. Broughton St., Historic District, 31401, tel. 912/644–7896 or 800/589–6304, fax 912/234–3334, www.marshallhouse.com. 65 rooms, 3 suites. Restaurant, lounge, meeting room. AE, D, MC, V.*

$$–$$$ **RIVER STREET INN.** The interior of this 1817 converted warehouse is so lavish that it's hard to believe the five-story building once stood vacant in a state of disrepair. Today the 86 guest rooms are filled with antiques and reproductions from the era of King Cotton. One floor has charming souvenir and gift shops and a New Orleans–style restaurant. *115 E. River St., Historic District, 31401, tel. 912/234–6400 or 800/678–8946, fax 912/234–1478, www.riverstreetinn.com. 86 rooms. 2 restaurants, 3 bars, shops, billiards, business services, meeting rooms. AE, D, DC, MC, V. BP.*

IN THIS CHAPTER

Updated by Hollis Gillespie

the coastal isles and the okefenokee

THE COASTAL ISLES ARE A STRING OF LUSH, SUBTROPICAL barrier islands meandering lazily down Georgia's Atlantic coast from Savannah to the Florida border. The islands have a long history of human habitation; Native American relics have been found here that date from about 2500 BC. The four designated Golden Isles—Little St. Simons Island, Sea Island, St. Simons Island, and Jekyll Island—are great vacation spots. The best way to appreciate the barrier islands' rare ecology is to visit Sapelo and Cumberland islands—part of Georgia's coastal isles—or to take a guided tour.

Each coastal isle has a distinct personality, shaped by its history and ecology. All the Golden Isles but Little St. Simons are connected to the mainland by bridges in the vicinity of Brunswick; these are the only coastal isles accessible by automobile. Little St. Simons Island, a privately owned retreat with guest accommodations, is reached by a launch from St. Simons. Sapelo Island is accessible by ferry from the visitor center just north of Darien (on the mainland). The Cumberland Island National Seashore is reached by ferry from St. Marys. About 60 mi inland is the Okefenokee National Wildlife Refuge, which has a character all its own.

The price categories for the Eating Out listings in this chapter refer to the following chart:

CATEGORY	COST*
$$$$	over $30
$$$	$20–$30
$$	$10–$20
$	under $10

*per person for a main course at dinner

Price categories for Where to Stay listings refer to the following chart:

CATEGORY	COST*
$$$$	over $175
$$$	$125–$175
$$	$75–$125
$	under $75

*All prices are for a standard double room, excluding 13% tax and service.

Lodging prices quoted here may be much lower during nonpeak seasons, and specials are often available during the week in high season. All Georgia beaches are in the public domain.

Numbers in the margin correspond to points of interest on the Coastal Isles map.

SAPELO ISLAND

 8 mi east of Darien.

In Sapelo's fields you might find chips of Guale Indian pottery dating as far back as 2000 BC and shards of Spanish ceramics from the 16th century. On the northern end, remains of the Chocolate Plantation recall the island's French heritage and role during the plantation days of the 19th century. Today researchers occupy the southern sector of the island, studying ecology at the Sapelo Island National Estuarine Research

the coastal isles

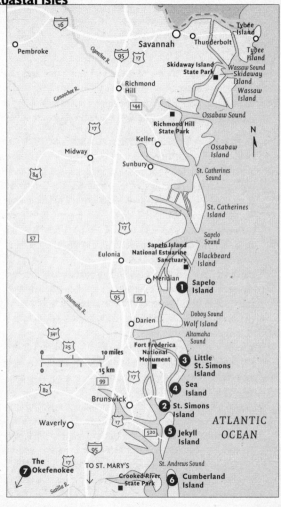

Reserve and evaluating the marshland at the Marine Institute. The organizations' studies are instrumental in preserving Sapelo's delicate ecosystem and others like it throughout the world.

You can explore many historical periods and natural environments here, but facilities on the island are limited for the most part to drinking fountains and rest rooms. Bring insect repellent, especially in summer, and leave your pets at home.

Start your visit at the **SAPELO ISLAND VISITORS CENTER** (Rte. 1, Box 1500, Darien 31305, tel. 912/437–3224; 912/485–2300 for group tours; 912/485–2299 for camping reservations, www.gacoast.com/navigator/sapelo.html). To get here from downtown Darien, go north on Route 99 for 8 mi, following signs for the Sapelo Island National Estuarine Research Reserve. At the visitor center you'll see an exhibition on the island's history, culture, and ecology. Here you can purchase a ticket good for a round-trip ferry ride and bus tour of the island. The sights that make up the bus tour vary depending on the day of the week, but always included are the marsh, the sand dune ecosystem, and the wildlife management area. On Saturday the tour includes the 80-ft **Sapelo Lighthouse,** built in 1820, a symbol of the cotton and lumber industry once based out of Darien's port. To see the island's **Reynolds Mansion,** schedule your tour for Wednesday. Reservations are required for tours. If you wish to stay overnight on Sapelo, you can either camp or choose from several B&B inns. If you stay overnight (and only if you do), you may visit the beach and, on a tour, the **Hog Hammock Community,** the few remaining sites on the south Atlantic coast where ethnic African-American culture has been preserved. Hog Hammock's 65 residents are descendants of slaves who worked the island's plantations during the 19th century. You can rent a bicycle at your hotel if you want to tour the area, but you cannot bring a bicycle on the ferry.

Eating Out and Where to Stay

$–$$ MUDCAT CHARLIE'S. It's plastic forks and plates all the way at this casual eatery. Local seafood—crab stew, fried oysters, and shrimp—is the specialty. The steaks, burgers, and pork chops are good, too. Peach and apple pies are made on the premises. It's between Brunswick and Darien on U.S. 17, 8 mi from Sapelo Island. *250 Ricefield Way, tel. 912/261–0055. AE, D, DC, MC, V.*

$$ OPEN GATES. Fine antiques fill the public spaces and guest rooms of this comfortable white-frame Victorian house, which dates from 1876. Breakfast specialties include fresh fig preserves, plantation (puffed) pancakes, and hunter's casserole (a baked egg strata). Innkeeper Carolyn Hodges offers guided tours of the Altamaha River. *Vernon Sq., Box 1526, Darien 31305, tel. 912/437–6985, fax 912/882–9427, www.opengatesbnb.com. 4 rooms, 2 with bath. Pool, library. No credit cards. BP.*

ST. SIMONS ISLAND

② *22 mi south of Darien, 6 mi south of Brunswick.*

As large as Manhattan, with more than 14,000 year-round residents, St. Simons is the Golden Isles' most complete resort destination. Fortunately, all this development has not spoiled the natural beauty of the island's regal live oaks, beaches, and salt marshes. Here you can swim and sun, golf, bike, hike, go fishing, horseback ride, tour historic sites, and feast on fresh local seafood at more than 50 restaurants.

Many sights and activities are in the **VILLAGE** area along Mallory Street at the more developed south end of the island, where you'll find shops, several restaurants, pubs, and a popular public pier. For $10 a quaint "trolley" takes you on a 1½-hour guided tour of the island, leaving from near the pier several times a day in high season; tours run less frequently in winter.

NEPTUNE PARK (550 Beachview Dr., tel. 912/638–2393), on the island's south end, has picnic tables, a children's play park, miniature golf, and beach access. A swimming pool ($3 per person), with showers and rest rooms, is open each summer in the **Neptune Park Casino.**

ST. SIMONS LIGHTHOUSE, a beacon since 1872, is virtually the symbol of St. Simons. The **Museum of Coastal History,** in the lightkeeper's cottage, has a permanent exhibit of coastal history. *101 12th St., tel. 912/638–4666, www.saintsimonslighthouse.org. $4, including lighthouse. Mon.–Sat. 10–5, Sun. 1:30–5.*

At the burgeoning north end of the island there's a marina, a golf club, and a housing development, as well as **FORT FREDERICA NATIONAL MONUMENT,** the ruins of a fort built by English troops in the mid-1730s as a bulwark against a Spanish invasion from Florida. Around the fort are the foundations of homes and shops. Start at the **National Park Service Visitors Center,** which has a film and displays. *Off Frederica Rd. just past Christ Episcopal Church, tel. 912/638–3639, www.nps.gov/fofr. $4 per car. Daily 8–5.*

Consecrated in 1886 following an earlier structure's desecration by Union troops, the white-frame Gothic-style **CHRIST EPISCOPAL CHURCH** is surrounded by live oaks, dogwoods, and azaleas. The interior has beautiful stained-glass windows. *6329 Frederica Rd., tel. 912/638–8683. Donations suggested.*

Eating Out and Where to Stay

$$–$$$$ **GEORGIA SEA GRILL.** This tiny and very popular place presents eclectic dishes, with fresh local seafood the house specialty. Standouts include tender shrimp au gratin, as well as fresh seafood prepared five different ways. Nightly specials are prepared personally by the chef–owners. *310B Mallory St., tel. 912/638–1197. D, MC, V. Closed Mon. May–Sept.; Sun.–Mon. Oct.–Apr. No lunch.*

$$–$$$ **CARGO PORTSIDE GRILL.** Don't miss this superb seaside pub, a short drive across the bridge in the small city of Brunswick. The

menu reads like a foodie's wish list, with succulent coastal and cross-coastal fare from many ports. All of it is creatively presented by owner–chef Alix Kanegy, formerly of Atlanta's Indigo Coastal Grill. Specials have included pasta Veracruz with grilled chicken, smoked tomatoes, poblano peppers, and caramelized onions in a chipotle cream sauce; in season, soft-shell crab is often on the menu. *1423 Newcastle St., Brunswick, tel. 912/267–7330. MC, V. Closed Sun.–Mon.*

$$–$$$ REDFERN CAFÉ. A popular spot with locals, the Redfern has up to six specials nightly in addition to the regular menu. Fried oysters in a light cornmeal coating, shrimp and crab bisque with corn fritters, and the crab cakes are specialties. *200 Redfern Village, tel. 912/634–1344. Reservations essential. MC, V. Closed Sun.*

~~Closed~~

638-2815

$–$$$ P. G. ARCHIBALD'S. In the village this lively restaurant and nightclub has a "bayou Victorian" style, with lots of antiques and memorabilia. The menu highlights seafood as well as basic steak and chicken dishes, plus oysters prepared 15 ways. Blue-crab soup is a local favorite, and the huge seafood platter could easily feed two. Open late, the restaurant also presents live entertainment Thursday through Saturday. *440 King's Way, tel. 912/638–3030. AE, DC, MC, V.*

$ RAFTERS BLUES CLUB, RESTAURANT AND RAW BAR. If you're looking for cheap, great food and a raucous good time, this place serves it up by the boatload. Revelers sit at long wooden-plank picnic tables and heartily partake in the offerings of both the prodigious bar and the equally generous kitchen. The restaurant serves ocean fare prepared in interesting ways—a seafood burrito, for example. Rafters is open late and presents live entertainment Wednesday through Saturday. *315½ Mallory St., tel. 912/634–9755. AE, D, MC, V. Closed Sun.*

$$$$ THE LODGE AT SEA ISLAND GOLF CLUB. This small but opulent lodge has assumed its place among the coast's most exclusive accommodations. Dashingly decorated rooms and suites all have water or golf-course views, and you can expect to be pampered by 24-hour butler service. You can also choose from among four stellar restaurants for dining. The lodge serves as the clubhouse for the Sea Island Golf Club (although this whole complex lies on St. Simons Island, so don't let the title disorient you) and encompasses a trophy room, locker rooms, and the Sea Island Golf Learning Center. *St. Simons Island 31522, tel. 912/638–3611 or 866/465–3563, www.golflodge.com. 40 rooms, 2 suites. 4 restaurants, bar, in-room VCRs, 2 18-hole golf courses, tennis court, pool, health club, hot tub, lounge, Internet, meeting room. AE, D, DC, MC, V.*

$$$ KING AND PRINCE BEACH AND GOLF RESORT. Most people who visit feel it's worth the expense to get a room with easy beach access at this cushy retreat. Guest rooms are spacious, and villas have two or three bedrooms. The villas are owned by private individuals, so the total number available for rent varies from time to time. *201 Arnold Rd., Box 20798, 31522, tel. 912/638–3631 or 800/342–0212, fax 912/634–1720, www.kingandprince.com. 148 rooms, 10 suites, 43 villas. 2 restaurants, bar, golf privileges, 2 tennis courts, 1 indoor and 4 outdoor pools, 3 hot tubs, bicycles, lounge, Internet. AE, D, MC, V.*

$$ HOLIDAY INN EXPRESS. With brightly decorated rooms at great prices, this nonsmoking facility is an excellent midprice option. The six King Executive rooms have sofas and desks. *Plantation Village, 299 Main St., 31522, tel. 912/634–2175 or 800/787–4666, fax 912/634–2174. 60 rooms. Cable TV, pool, bicycles, laundry service, meeting room. AE, D, MC, V.*

$–$$ SEA PALMS GOLF AND TENNIS RESORT. Given this resort's emphasis on golf and tennis, it's an ideal milieu if you're the sports-minded type. Rooms have balconies overlooking the golf course, and they are large—so large they're touted as the biggest standard guest rooms in the Golden Isles. The furnishings are somewhat unimaginative, however. This is a contemporary complex with fully furnished villas (suites), most with kitchens, nestled on an 800-acre site. Guests also enjoy beach club privileges. *5445 Frederica Rd., 31522, tel. 912/638–3351 or 800/841–6268, fax 912/634–*

8029, www.seapalms.com. 149 rooms, 26 suites. 2 restaurants, bar, 27-hole golf course, 3 tennis courts, 2 pools, health club, bicycles, volleyball, children's programs, convention center. AE, DC, MC, V.

RENTALS

For St. Simons condo and cottage rentals, contact **GOLDEN ISLES REALTY** (330 Mallory St., 31522, tel. 912/638–8623 or 800/337–3106, fax 912/638–6925). **TRUPP-HODNETT ENTERPRISES** (520 Ocean Blvd., 31522, tel. 912/638–5450 or 800/627–6850, fax 912/638–2983) provides boat rentals.

LITTLE ST. SIMONS ISLAND

3 10–15 mins by ferry from the Hampton River Club Marina on St. Simons Island.

Six miles long, 2–3 mi wide, and skirted by Atlantic beaches and salt marshes teeming with birds and wildlife, this privately owned resort is custom-made for Robinson Crusoe–style getaways. The island's only development is a rustic but comfortable guest compound. Guided tours, horseback rides, canoe trips, fly-fishing lessons, and other extras can be arranged, some for no additional charge. Inquire about the advisability of bringing children, as there are some limitations. In summer day tours can be arranged.

The island's forests and marshes are inhabited by deer, armadillos, horses, raccoons, gators, otters, and more than 200 species of birds. As a guest you're free to walk the 6 mi of undisturbed beaches, swim in the mild surf, fish from the dock, and seine (you and others take a net, walk into the ocean, and drag the net back to shore) for shrimp and crabs in the marshes. There are also horses to ride, nature walks with experts, and other island explorations via boat or the back of the hotel's pickup truck. From June through September up to 10 nonguests per day may visit the island by reservation; the $75 cost includes the ferry to the island, an island tour by truck, lunch at the lodge, and a beach walk. Contact the Lodge on Little St. Simons Island for more information.

Eating Out and Where to Stay

$$$$ **LODGE ON LITTLE ST. SIMONS ISLAND.** This gorgeous resort cites full capacity at a mere 30 guests. Meals are included—platters are heaped with fresh fish, homemade breads, and pies. You also get complimentary drinks during cocktail hour. Transportation from St. Simons Island, transportation on the island, and interpretive guides are also provided. Box 21078, 31522, tel. 912/638–7472 or 888/733–5774, fax 912/634–1811, www.littlestsimonsisland.com. 14 rooms, 1 suite. Restaurant, pool, beach, boating, fishing, bicycles, horseback riding. AE, D, MC, V. FAP.

SEA ISLAND

4 5 mi northeast of St. Simons Island.

Separated from St. Simons Island by a narrow waterway and a good many steps on the social ladder, Sea Island has been the domain of the well-heeled and the Cloister Hotel since 1928. There is no entrance gate, and nonguests are free to admire the beautifully planted grounds and to drive past the mansions lining Sea Island Drive. The owners of the 180 or so private cottages and villas treat the hotel like a country club, and their tenants may use the hotel's facilities. For rentals contact **SEA ISLAND COTTAGE RENTALS** (Box 30351, 31561, tel. 912/638–5112 or 800/732–4752, fax 912/638–5824).

Where to Stay

$$$$ **THE CLOISTER.** The Cloister undeniably lives up to its celebrity status as a grand coastal resort. You can get a spacious, comfortably appointed room or suite in the Spanish Mediterranean–style hotel—designed by Florida architect Addison Mizner—or in the

property's later-built Ocean Houses, which offer 56 dramatic suites connected by lavish house parlors with fireplaces and staffed bars. The state-of-the-art spa at the Cloister is in a beautiful building all its own. You also get access to the nearby Sea Island Golf Course. *Sea Island 31561, tel. 912/638–3611 or 800/732–4752, fax 912/638–5823, www.cloister.com. 274 rooms, 32 suites. 4 restaurants, bar, cable TV, 3 18-hole golf courses, 18 tennis courts, 2 pools, health club, spa, bicycles, 2 lounges, children's programs, business services, airport shuttle. AE, D, DC, MC, V. FAP.*

JEKYLL ISLAND

⑤ *18 mi south of St. Simons Island, 90 mi south of Savannah.*

For 56 winters, between 1886 and 1942, America's rich and famous faithfully came south to Jekyll Island. Through the Gilded Age, the Great War, as World War I was originally known, the Roaring '20s, and the Great Depression, Vanderbilts and Rockefellers, Morgans and Astors, Macys, Pulitzers, and Goodyears shuttered their 5th Avenue castles and retreated to the serenity of their wild Georgia island. Here they built elegant "cottages," played golf and tennis, and socialized. Early in World War II the millionaires departed for the last time. In 1947 the state of Georgia purchased the entire island for the bargain price of $675,000.

Jekyll Island is still a 7½-mi playground but is no longer restricted to the rich and famous. The golf, tennis, fishing, biking, and jogging, the water park, and the picnic grounds are open to all. One side of the island is lined by nearly 10 mi of hard-packed Atlantic beaches; the other, by the Intracoastal Waterway and picturesque salt marshes. Deer and wild turkeys inhabit interior forests of pine, magnolia, and moss-veiled live oaks. Egrets, pelicans, herons, and sandpipers skim the gentle surf. Jekyll's clean, mostly uncommercialized public beaches are free and open year-round. Bathhouses with rest rooms, changing areas, and showers are open at regular intervals along the beach. Beachwear, suntan lotion, rafts, snacks, and drinks are available at the **Jekyll Shopping Center,** facing the beach at Beachview Drive.

The **JEKYLL ISLAND MUSEUM VISITOR CENTER** gives tram tours of the Jekyll Island National Historic Landmark District. Tours originate at the museum's visitor center on Stable Road and include several millionaires' residences in the 240-acre historic district. Faith Chapel, illuminated by Tiffany stained-glass windows, is open for meditation daily 2–4. *381 Riverview Dr., I–95, Exit 29, tel. 912/635–2762 or 800/841–6586, fax 912/635–4004. $10. Daily 9–5, tours daily 10–3.*

Eating Out and Where to Stay

$$$ **GRAND DINING ROOM.** In the Jekyll Island Club Hotel, the dining
★ room sparkles with silver and crystal. The cuisine reflects the elegance of the private hunting club that flourished from the late 19th century to the World War II era and which brought a fine chef and staff in from New York's Delmonico's. Enjoy the blue-crab cakes, grilled pork with Vidalia onion, and local seafood. The restaurant has its own label pinot noir and chardonnay, made by Mountain View Vineyards. *371 Riverview Dr., Jekyll Island Club Hotel, tel. 912/635–2600. Reservations essential. AE, D, DC, MC, V.*

$$ **COURTYARD AT CRANE.** This notable addition to the island's restaurant scene offers alfresco dining in the courtyard of Crane Cottage, part of the Jekyll Island Club Hotel. The menu focuses on creative salads and entrées inspired by the world-famous kitchens of the Napa/Sonoma Valley wine country. You might sample the Mediterranean platter of grilled vegetables, imported olives, and fresh mozzarella with *crostini;* or a lobster-salad croissant with avocado, red onion, apple-wood-smoked bacon, tomato, and alfalfa sprouts. *371 Riverview Dr., Jekyll Island Club Hotel, tel. 912/635–2600. AE, D, DC, MC, V. Closed Sun.*

$$ **SEAJAY'S WATERFRONT CAFE & PUB.** Convivial and festive, with a swamp-shack style, this tavern serves delicious—and inexpensive—seafood, including a crab chowder that locals love. This is also the home of a wildly popular shrimp-boil buffet: a Lowcountry all-you-can-eat feast of local shrimp, corn on the cob, smoked sausage, and new potatoes served in a pot. *Jekyll Harbor Marina, tel. 912/635–3200. AE, MC, V.*

$$$–$$$$ **JEKYLL ISLAND CLUB HOTEL.** This sprawling 1886 resort, the
★ focal point of which is a four-story clubhouse—with couches and a fireplace—has wraparound verandas and Queen Anne–style towers and turrets. Guest rooms, suites, apartments, and cottages are custom-decorated with mahogany beds, armoires, and plush sofas and chairs. Two beautifully restored former "millionaires' cottages"—the Crane Cottage and the Cherokee Cottage—add 23 elegant guest rooms to this gracefully groomed compound. Note the B&B packages—they're a great deal. *371 Riverview Dr., 31527, tel. 912/635–2600 or 800/535–9547, fax 912/635–2818, www.jekyllclub.com. 139 rooms, 15 suites. 3 restaurants, bar, cable TV, 13 tennis courts, pool, beach, bicycles, croquet, lounge, Internet, meeting room. AE, D, DC, MC, V.*

$$–$$$$ **BEACHVIEW CLUB.** They literally raised the roof on an old motel
★ to build this luxury all-suites lodging. Stucco walls are painted light yellow, and big old oak trees shade the grounds. Efficiencies have either one king- or two queen-size beds, a desk, and a kitchenette. All rooms either are on the oceanfront or have at least a partial ocean view from the balcony, and some rooms are equipped with a hot tub and gas fireplace. The interior design reflects an understated island theme. An attempt to target the corporate crowd has proven effective, and the unique meeting room in the Bell Tower accommodates up to 35 people for business events. Higher-end suites have full kitchens. *721 N. Beachview Dr., 31527, tel. 912/635–2256 or 800/299–2228, fax 912/635–3770, www.beachviewclub.com. 21 efficiencies, 7 suites. Restaurant, bar, some kitchenettes, microwaves, pool, hot tub, Internet, meeting room. AE, D, DC, MC, V.*

\$\$–\$\$\$ HOLIDAY INN BEACH RESORT. Amid natural dunes and oaks in a secluded oceanfront location, this hotel has a private beach. Each room has a balcony, but none has an ocean view (though it's a short walk away). The boardwalk out to the beach meanders through a lovely regional landscape, thick with palm trees and other native flora. *200 S. Beachview Dr., 31527, tel. 912/635–3311 or 800/753–5955, fax 912/635–2901, www.sixcontinentshotels.com. 198 rooms. Restaurant, bar, 2 tennis courts, pool, health club, bicycles, lobby lounge, playground. AE, D, DC, MC, V.*

\$–\$\$ JEKYLL INN. This popular oceanfront spread's 15 verdant acres space the buildings generously apart. Popular with families, the inn accommodates children under 17 free when they stay with parents or grandparents. Packages include summer family-focused arrangements and romantic getaways. The Italian restaurant offers basic, hearty fare. *975 N. Beachview Dr., 31527, tel. 912/635–2531 or 800/431–5190, fax 912/635–2332, www.jekyllinn.com. 188 rooms, 66 villas. Restaurant, 2 bars, refrigerators, pool, volleyball, lobby lounge, playground, children's programs, laundry service, meeting room. AE, D, DC, MC, V.*

RENTALS

Jekyll's more than 200 rental cottages and condos are handled by **JEKYLL REALTY** (Box 13096, 31527, tel. 912/635–3301 or 888/333–5055, fax 912/635–3303). **PARKER-KAUFMAN REALTY** (Box 13126, 31527, tel. 912/635–2512 or 888/453–5955, fax 912/635–2190) is a small outfit that provides cottage and condo rental information.

Outdoor Activities and Sports

GOLF

The **JEKYLL ISLAND GOLF CLUB** (322 Capt. Wylly Rd., tel. 912/635–2368) has 63 holes, including three 18-hole, par-72 courses, and a clubhouse. Greens fees are \$35, good all day, and carts are \$14.50 per person per course. There's also a 9-hole, par-36 course, the **Historic Oceanside Nine** (N. Beachview Dr., tel. 912/635–2170), where the millionaires used to play. Greens fees are $21, and carts are $7.25 for every 9 holes.

NATURE CENTER

The **COASTAL ENCOUNTERS NATURE CENTER** runs summer programs for children and families on the ecology of the coastal islands. Programs and excursions are individually priced. At the center are exhibits about the fauna of the region. 100 S. Riverview Dr., tel. 912/635–9102, http://coastalgeorgia.com/coastalencounters. Donation. Mon.–Sat. 9–5.

TENNIS

The **JEKYLL ISLAND TENNIS CENTER** (400 Capt. Wylly Rd., tel. 912/635–3154) has 13 clay courts, with seven lighted for nighttime play; it hosts eight USTA-sanctioned tournaments throughout the year. Costs are $14 per hour daily 9–6 and $16 per hour for lighted courts (available until 10 PM); reservations for lighted courts are required and must be made prior to 6 PM the day of play.

WATER PARK

SUMMER WAVES, an 11-acre water park, has an 18,000-square-ft wave pool, water slides, a children's activity pool with two slides, and a circular river for tubing and rafting. You are not permitted to bring your own equipment. 210 S. Riverview Dr., tel. 912/635–2074, www.summerwaves.com. $14.95. Late May–early Sept. (and some additional weekends in early May and late Sept.), Sun.–Fri. 10–6, Sat. 10–8 (hrs vary at beginning and end of season).

CUMBERLAND ISLAND

6 47 mi south of Jekyll Island, 115 mi south of Savannah to St. Marys via I–95, 45 mins by ferry from St. Marys.

The largest, most southerly, and most accessible of Georgia's primitive coastal islands is Cumberland Island, a 16- by 3-mi sanctuary of marshes, dunes, beaches, forests, lakes and ponds, estuaries, and inlets. Waterways are homes for gators, sea turtles, otters, snowy egrets, great blue herons, ibises, wood storks, and more than 300 other species of birds. In the forests are armadillos, wild horses, deer, raccoons, and an assortment of reptiles.

After the ancient Guale Indians came 16th-century Spanish missionaries, 18th-century English soldiers, and 19th-century planters. During the 1880s the Thomas Carnegie family (he was the brother of industrialist Andrew) of Pittsburgh built several lavish homes here, but the island remained largely as nature created it. In the early 1970s the federal government established the **CUMBERLAND ISLAND NATIONAL SEASHORE** and opened this natural treasure to the public. There is no transportation on the island itself, and the only public access to the island is via the *Cumberland Queen*, a reservations-only, 146-passenger ferry based near the National Park Service Information Center at St. Marys. Ferry bookings are heavy in summer, but cancellations and no-shows often make last-minute space available. Reservations may be made up to 11 months in advance.

From the park-service docks at the island's south end, you can follow wooded nature trails, swim and sun on 18 mi of undeveloped beaches, go fishing and bird-watching, and view the ruins of Thomas Carnegie's great estate, **Dungeness.** You can also join history and nature walks led by park-service rangers. Bear in mind that summers are hot and humid and that you must bring everything you need, including your own food, soft drinks, sunscreen, and a reliable insect repellent. *Cumberland Island National Seashore, Box 806, 31558, tel. 912/882–4335, fax 912/673–7747, www.nps.gov/cuis. Round-trip ferry $12, day pass $4, annual pass $20. Mid-May–Sept., ferry departure from St. Marys daily at 9 and 11:45, from Cumberland Mar.–Nov., Wed.–Sat. at 10:15, 2:45, and 4:45, Sun.–Tues. at 10:15 and 4:45. No ferry service Dec.–Feb., Tues.–Wed.*

Eating Out and Where to Stay

ISLAND

$$$$ **GREYFIELD INN.** Cumberland Island's only accommodations are in a turn-of-the-20th-century Carnegie family home. Greyfield's public areas are filled with family mementos, furnishings, and portraits (you may feel as though you've stepped into one of Agatha Christie's mysterious Cornwall manors). Prices include all meals, transportation, tours led by a naturalist, and bike rentals.8 N. 2nd St., Box 900, Fernandina Beach, FL 32035, tel. 904/261–6408, fax 904/321–0666, www.greyfieldinn.com. 13 rooms, 4 suites. Restaurant, bar, bicycle rentals. AE, D, MC, V. FAP.

$ ⛺ **CAMPING.** The island has three primitive camping sites in a National Wilderness Area. Reservations are required for all camping at these sites, and the rate is $2 per person per day. To reach the sites (Hickory Hill, Yankee Paradise, and Brickhill Bluff), start north of Sea Camp dock and then hike (with all equipment) from 4 to 10 mi. Equipment must include rope to suspend provisions from trees for critter control. Nonwilderness Stafford Beach is good for novice backpackers. A half mile from the dock, with rest rooms and showers adjacent to campsites, Sea Camp is the ideal spot for first-time campers ($4 per person per day). Also available are 16 campsites that can accommodate a maximum of 60 persons. Reservations are required (recommended at least two months in advance), no pets or fires are allowed, and a seven-day stay is the limit. Bring all required equipment. The beach is just beyond the dunes. To make a reservation, contact the Cumberland Island National Seashore.

MAINLAND

$$ **GREEK MEDITERRANEAN GRILL.** It's a block from the St. Marys River, but the sky-blue murals and Greek proprietors make it seem more like the Mediterranean than the South. Traditional Greek dishes, such as *pastitsio* (pasta and ground beef baked with cinnamon and white cream sauce) and moussaka, are the mainstay. 122 Osborne St., St. Marys, tel. 912/576–2000. No credit cards.

$$–$$$ SPENCER HOUSE INN. This comfortable Victorian inn dates from 1872 and is named for the sea captain who built it as a hotel. Some rooms have expansive balconies that overlook the neatly tended grounds; others have antique claw-foot bathtubs. Innkeepers Mike and Mary Neff reside here and will prepare picnic lunches if you ask. The inn makes a perfect base for a tour of historic St. Marys and the waterfront and is convenient to the *Cumberland Queen* ferry. 200 Osborne St., St. Marys 31558, tel. 912/882–1872, fax 912/882–9427, www.spencerhouseinn.com. 13 rooms, 1 suite. No room phones, no room TVs. AE, D, MC, V. BP.

OKEFENOKEE NATIONAL WILDLIFE REFUGE

★ ⑦ *65 mi southwest of Brunswick, 42 mi west of St. Marys.*

Covering 730 square mi of southeastern Georgia and spilling over into northeastern Florida, the **OKEFENOKEE,** with its mysterious rivers and lakes, bristles with seen and unseen life. Scientists agree that the Okefenokee, the largest intact freshwater wetlands in the contiguous United States, is not duplicated anywhere else on earth. The impenetrable Pinhook Swamp, to the south, part of the same ecosystem, adds another 100 square mi. If the term *swamp* denotes a dark, dank place, the Okefenokee is never that. Instead, it is a vast peat bog with numerous and varied landscapes, including aquatic prairies, towering virgin cypress, sandy pine islands, and lush subtropical hammocks. During the last Ice Age 10,000 years ago, it was part of the ocean flow. Peat began building up 7,000 years ago atop a mound of clay, now 120 ft above sea level. Two rivers, the St. Marys and the Suwanee, flow out of the refuge, and it provides at least a part-time habitat for myriad species of birds, mammals, reptiles, amphibians, and fish.

As you travel by canoe or speedboat among the water lilies and the great stands of live oaks and cypress, be on the lookout for, among many others, alligators, otters, bobcats, raccoons, opossums, white-tailed deer, turtles, bald eagles, red-tailed hawks, egrets, muskrats, herons, cranes, and red-cockaded woodpeckers. The black bears tend to be more reclusive.

The Seminole people, in their migrations south toward Florida's Everglades, once took refuge in the Okefenokee. The last Native Americans to occupy the area, they were evicted by the army and Georgia's militia in the 1830s. When the Okefenokee acquired its present status of federal preserve (1937), the white homesteaders living on its fringe were forced out.

Noting the many floating islands, the Seminole named this unique combination of land and water "Land of the Quivering Earth." If you have the rare fortune to walk one of these bogs, you will find the earth does indeed quiver, rather like fruit gelatin in a bowl.

The Okefenokee Swamp Park, 8 mi south of Waycross, is a nonprofit development. The northern entrance to the refuge is here. There are two other gateways to the swamp: an eastern entrance at the U.S. Fish and Wildlife Service headquarters in the Suwanee Canal Recreation Area, near Folkston; and a western entrance at Stephen C. Foster State Park, outside the town of Fargo. You may take an overnight canoeing-camping trip into the interior, but the Okefenokee is a wildlife refuge and designated national wilderness, not a park. Access is restricted by permit. The best way to see the Okefenokee up close is to take a day trip at one of the three gateways. Plan your visit between September and April to avoid the biting insects that emerge in May, especially in the dense interior.

South of Waycross, via U.S. 1, **OKEFENOKEE SWAMP PARK** has orientation programs, exhibits, a 1⅓-mi nature trail, observation areas, wilderness walkways, an outdoor museum of pioneer life, and boat tours into the swamp that reveal its unique ecology. A boardwalk and 90-ft tower are excellent places to glimpse cruising gators and birds. You may arrange for guided boat tours at an additional cost. A 1½-mi train tour passes by a Seminole village and stops at Pioneer Island, a re-created pioneer homestead, for a 30-minute walking tour. *5700 Swamp Park Rd., Waycross 31501, tel. 912/283–0583, fax 912/283–0023, www.okefenokee.com. $10, plus $4–$8 extra for boat-tour packages. Daily 8–5.*

STEPHEN C. FOSTER STATE PARK, 18 mi northeast of Fargo via Route 177, is an 80-acre island park within the Okefenokee National Wildlife Refuge. The park encompasses a large cypress-and-black-gum forest, a majestic backdrop for one of the thickest growths of vegetation in the southeastern United States. Park naturalists leading boat tours will spill out a wealth of Okefenokee lore while you observe alligators, birds, and native trees and plants. You may also take a self-guided excursion in rental canoes and a motorized flat-bottom boat. Campsites and cabins are available. *Rte. 1, Box 131, Fargo 31631, tel. 912/637–5274. $5 per vehicle to National Wildlife Refuge.*

SUWANEE CANAL RECREATION AREA, 8 mi southwest of Folkston via Route 121, is administered by the U.S. Fish and Wildlife Service. Stop first at the visitor center, with exhibits on the Okefenokee's flora and fauna. A boardwalk takes you over the water to a 50-ft observation tower. The concession has equipment rentals and daily food service; you may sign up here for one- or two-hour guided boat tours. Hikers, bicyclists, and private motor vehicles are welcome on the Swamp Island Drive; several interpretive walking trails may be taken along the way. Picnicking is allowed. Wilderness canoeing and camping in the Okefenokee's interior are by reserved permit only (for which a fee is charged). Permits are hard to get, especially in cool weather. Call **refuge headquarters** (tel. 912/496–3331) when it opens at 7 AM *exactly* two months in advance of your desired starting date. Guided overnight canoe trips can be arranged by refuge concessionaire Carl E. Glenn Jr. *Rte. 2, Box 3325, Folkston 31537, tel. 912/496–7156; Refuge headquarters: Rte. 2, Box 3330, Folkston 31537, tel. 912/496–7836. $5 per car; 1-hr tours $11; 2-hr* tours $19. *Refuge Mar.–Sept. 10, daily 6:30 AM–7:30 PM; Sept. 11–Feb., daily 8–6.*

Where to Stay

$$–$$$ **THE INN AT FOLKSTON.** This craftsman-style inn, just 7 mi from the refuge, has a huge front veranda and four working gas-log fireplaces. Guest rooms are individually decorated. The romantic Lighthouse Room, for example, has a king-size bed and screened-in porch with a fireplace. The Garden Room woos romantics with a whirlpool tub, and the Oriental Room has an Asian theme. *509 W. Main St., Folkston 31537, tel. 912/496–6256 or 888/509–6246, www.innatfolkston.com. 4 rooms. Hot tub, library. AE, MC, V. BP.*

$ ⚠ **LAURA S. WALKER STATE PARK.** Named for a Waycross teacher who championed conservation, the park, 9 mi northeast of Okefenokee Swamp Park, has campsites with electrical and water hookups. Be sure to pick up food and supplies on the way to the park. Boating and skiing are permitted on the 120-acre lake, and there's an 18-hole championship golf course. Rustic cabins cost $21.40 per night, plus $2 parking. *5500 Laura Walker Rd., Waycross 31503, tel. 912/287–4900 or 800/864–7275. 44 campsites. Picnic area, pool, fishing, playground.*

$ ⚠ **STEPHEN C. FOSTER STATE PARK.** The park has two-room furnished cottages, each capable of sleeping eight, and campsites with water, electricity, rest rooms, and showers. Because of roaming wildlife and poachers and because of the park's location inside the refuge, the gates close between sunset and sunrise. If you're staying overnight, stop for groceries before you get here. Cottages cost $66–$86 per night, depending on the season. *Fargo 31631, tel. 912/637–5274 or 800/864–7275. 66 campsites.*

IN THIS CHAPTER

Updated by Mary Sue Lawrence

charleston

AT FIRST GLIMPSE Charleston resembles an 18th-century etching come to life. Its low-profile skyline is punctuated with the spires and steeples of 181 churches, representing 25 denominations—the reason that Charleston, known for religious freedom during its formation, is called the Holy City. Parts of the city appear frozen in time; block after block of old downtown structures have been preserved and restored for residential and commercial use, and some brick and cobblestone streets remain. Charleston has survived three centuries of epidemics, earthquakes, fires, and hurricanes, and it is today one of the South's loveliest and best-preserved cities. It is not a museum, however: throughout the year festivals add excitement and sophistication.

Besides the historic district (which we've divided, for ease of exploration, into two parts: the area north of Broad Street, and the Battery and area south of Broad Street), a visit to the city can easily include nearby towns, plantations and outstanding gardens, and historic sites, whether in Mount Pleasant or the area west of the Ashley River.

HERE AND THERE

NORTH OF BROAD

To really appreciate Charleston, you must walk its streets. The downtown historic district, roughly bounded by Calhoun Street to the north, the Cooper River to the east, the Battery to the south, and Legare Street to the west, is large, with 2,000 historic homes and buildings on the southeastern tip of the Charleston peninsula. In a fairly compact area you'll find churches, museums, and lovely views at every turn.

The area north of Broad Street has some of the finest historic homes and neighborhoods in the city, including the Mazyck/Wraggborough neighborhood, where you'll find the Aiken-Rhett House. Large tracts of land made this area ideal for urban plantations during the early 1800s. Although there are a number of prerevolutionary buildings here (including the Old Powder Magazine, the oldest public building in Charleston), in general, the farther north you travel on the peninsula, the newer the development. Still, because the peninsula was built-out by the early 1900s, North of Broad is rich with historic buildings from the 19th century and can be lovely—especially since most tourists are busy conquering the waterfront area.

Numbers in the text correspond to numbers in the margin and on the Charleston map.

A Good Walk

Before you begin touring, drop by the **VISITOR INFORMATION CENTER** ① on Meeting Street for an overview of the city, a map, and tickets for shuttle services if you want to give your feet a break. Start across the street at the **CHARLESTON MUSEUM** ②, with its large decorative arts collection; then turn right on Ann Street and follow it to Elizabeth Street to the palatial **AIKEN-RHETT HOUSE** ③. After touring the house, head south down Elizabeth Street and turn right on John Street for the **JOSEPH MANIGAULT MANSION** ④, another impressive house museum dating to the early 1800s. Continue on John Street to reach the **AMERICAN MILITARY MUSEUM** ⑤. Return to Meeting Street and walk south toward Calhoun Street, passing the **OLD CITADEL BUILDING** ⑥, converted into an Embassy Suites. Take a left on Calhoun Street; a half block down on your left is the **EMANUEL AFRICAN METHODIST EPISCOPAL CHURCH** ⑦,

charleston

where slave rebellion leader Denmark Vesey was a member. From here you may want to use the shuttle bus DASH to give your feet a rest, or cross the street to Marion Square Mall for a drink and a break.

Retrace your steps on Calhoun Street (passing the Francis Marion Hotel, in the 1920s the highest building in the Carolinas) and continue two blocks west to St. Phillips Street, where you turn left to end up in the midst of the romantic campus of the **COLLEGE OF CHARLESTON** ⑧, the oldest municipal college in the country. Enter through one of the gated openings on St. Phillips Street for a stroll under the many moss-draped trees. Then head east to King Street, Charleston's main shopping thoroughfare, and turn right; turn left on Hasell Street to see **KAHAL KADOSH BETH ELOHIM REFORM TEMPLE** ⑨, a Greek Revival building. Across the street is **ST. MARY'S CATHOLIC CHURCH** ⑩. Keep walking down Hasell Street and turn right on Meeting Street. Two blocks to the south are **MARKET HALL** ⑪ and the bustling **OLD CITY MARKET** ⑫. Now is a good time for a carriage tour, many of which leave from here. Across Meeting Street is the classy **CHARLESTON PLACE** ⑬, with its graceful hotel and cluster of shops. You can browse from one end to the other, exiting on King Street.

Cross the street and walk a block down Market Street, turning left on quiet Archdale Street to wander through **ST. JOHN'S LUTHERAN CHURCH** ⑭ and the peaceful graveyard of the **UNITARIAN CHURCH** ⑮. Turn left on Queen Street at the bottom of Archdale and walk two blocks to Meeting Street, where you turn left for the **GIBBES MUSEUM OF ART** ⑯, with its spectacular stained-glass dome. Across the street is the **CIRCULAR CONGREGATIONAL CHURCH** ⑰. Behind it, on Cumberland Street, is the **OLD POWDER MAGAZINE** ⑱. To the left as you face the building, you'll catch a glimpse of the steeple of **ST. PHILIP'S EPISCOPAL CHURCH** ⑲, famous in the city's skyline; it's around the corner on Church Street.

Cross over to picturesque Church Street to the **FRENCH PROTESTANT (HUGUENOT) CHURCH** ⑳ and the **DOCK STREET THEATRE** ㉑, across the street. You might detour east here, down Queen Street and along Vendue Range to **WATERFRONT PARK** ㉒, to relax in a bench swing overlooking beautiful river views, dramatic fountains, and a fishing pier.

TIMING

Set aside from two to four hours for this walk, depending on your pace. Most of the house-museum tours last about 40 minutes, so you might choose the two or three that interest you most. Charleston rickshaws (bicycle-powered two-seaters), which can take you anywhere downtown for $6, can ease the trip back.

What to See

❸ **AIKEN-RHETT HOUSE.** This stately 1819 mansion, with its original wallpaper, paint colors, and some of its furnishings, was the headquarters of Confederate general P. G. T. Beauregard during his 1864 Civil War defense of Charleston. The house, kitchen, slave quarters, and work yard are maintained much as they were when the original occupants lived here, making this one of the most complete examples of African-American urban life of the period. *48 Elizabeth St., Upper King, tel. 843/723–1159, www. historiccharleston.org. $7; combination ticket with Nathaniel Russell House $12. Mon.–Sat. 10–5, Sun. 2–5.*

🕐 ❺ **AMERICAN MILITARY MUSEUM.** The museum displays hundreds of uniforms and artifacts from all branches of service, beginning with the Revolutionary War. Its collections also include antique toy soldiers, war toys, miniatures, and weaponry. *44 John St., Upper King, tel. 843/723–9620. $5. Mon.–Sat. 10–6, Sun. 1–6.*

★ 🕐 ❷ **CHARLESTON MUSEUM.** Founded in 1773, the country's oldest city museum is in a contemporary complex. The 500,000 items in the collection—in addition to Charleston silver, fashions, toys, snuffboxes, and the like—include objects relating to natural history, archaeology, and ornithology. Its South Carolina decorative arts holdings are extraordinary. The Discover Me Room, designed just for children, has computers and other hands-on exhibits. Two historic homes—the **Joseph Manigault Mansion** and the **Heyward-Washington House**—are owned and managed by the museum. *360 Meeting St., Upper King, tel. 843/722–2996, www. charlestonmuseum.com. $8; museum and houses $18; 2 of the 3 sights $12. Mon.–Sat. 9–5, Sun. 1–5.*

⑬ CHARLESTON PLACE. The city's only world-class hotel, this Orient-Express property is flanked by a complex of upscale boutiques and specialty shops. Peek into the lobby or have cocktails or tea in the intimate Lobby Lounge. Entrances for the garage and reception area are on Hasell Street between Meeting and King streets. *130 Market St., Market area, tel. 843/722–4900.*

⑰ CIRCULAR CONGREGATIONAL CHURCH. The corners of this unusual Romanesque church were rounded off, they say, so the devil would have no place to hide. Simple but pretty, it has a beamed, vaulted ceiling. *150 Meeting St., Market area, tel. 843/ 577–6400. Call for tour schedule.*

⑧ COLLEGE OF CHARLESTON. The lovely, tree-shaded campus of this college, founded in 1770, has a graceful main building, the Randolph House (1828), designed by Philadelphia architect William Strickland. It's a romantic backdrop for the Cistern, often used as a grassy stage for concerts and other activities. Within the college, centered at the corner of George and St. Phillips streets in what was once a school for freed slaves, is the **Avery Research Center for African-American History and Culture,** which traces the heritage of Lowcountry African-Americans. Civil Rights activist Cleveland Seller's personal letters, telegrams, newspaper clippings, and other papers—one of the best series of manuscript collections documenting the Civil Rights movement—is here. *Avery Research Center, 125 Bull St., College of Charleston Campus, tel. 843/953–7609, www.cofc.edu/~averyrsc. Free. Mon.–Sat. noon–5, mornings by appointment.*

㉑ DOCK STREET THEATRE. Built on the site of one of the nation's first playhouses, the building combines the reconstructed early Georgian playhouse and the preserved Old Planter's Hotel (circa 1809). The theater, which offers fascinating backstage views, welcomes visitors except when technical work for a show is under way. *135 Church St., Market area, tel. 843/720–3968. Free tours; call ahead for ticket prices and performance times. Weekdays 10–4.*

❼ EMANUEL AFRICAN METHODIST EPISCOPAL CHURCH. Home of the South's oldest A.M.E. congregation, the church had its beginnings in 1818. It was closed in 1822 when authorities learned that Denmark Vesey had used the sanctuary to plan his slave insurrection, but the church reopened in 1865 at the present site. *110 Calhoun St., Upper King, tel. 843/722–2561. Daily 9–4.*

⓴ FRENCH PROTESTANT (HUGUENOT) CHURCH. This church is the only one in the country still using the original Huguenot liturgy, which can be heard in a special service held each spring. *110 Church St., Market area, tel. 843/722–4385. Weekdays 10–12:30 and 2–4.*

⓰ GIBBES MUSEUM OF ART. The collections of American art include notable 18th- and 19th-century portraits of Carolinians and an outstanding group of more than 400 miniature portraits. Don't miss the miniature rooms—intricately detailed with fabrics and furnishings and nicely displayed in shadowboxes inset in dark-paneled walls—or the Tiffany-style stained-glass dome in the rotunda. *135 Meeting St., Market area, tel. 843/722–2706, www. gibbes.com. $5. Tues.–Sat. 10–5, Sun.–Mon. 1–5.*

NEED A
BREAK?
Just across the street from the Gibbes Museum, **JOSEPH'S** (129 Meeting St., Market area, tel. 843/958–8500) serves a great Southern breakfast, lovely lunch, and super Sunday brunch in its courtyard garden.

❹ JOSEPH MANIGAULT MANSION. A National Historic Landmark and an outstanding example of neoclassical architecture, this home was designed by Charleston architect Gabriel Manigault in 1803 and is noted for its carved-wood mantels and elaborate plasterwork. Some furnishings are British and French, but most are Charleston antiques; some rare tricolor Wedgwood pieces are noteworthy. *350 Meeting St., Upper King, tel. 843/723–2926, www.charlestonmuseum.com. $7; museum and houses $18; 2 of the 3 sights $12. Mon.–Sat. 10–5, Sun. 1–5.*

❾ KAHAL KADOSH BETH ELOHIM REFORM TEMPLE. Considered one of the nation's finest examples of Greek Revival architecture, this temple was built in 1840 to replace an earlier one—the birthplace of American reform Judaism in 1824—that was destroyed by fire. *86 Hasell St., Market area, tel. 843/723–1090, www.kkbe.org. Weekdays 10–noon.*

⓫ MARKET HALL. Built in 1841 and modeled after the Temple of Nike in Athens, this imposing landmark, now open after a five-year renovation, includes the **Confederate Museum,** where the Daughters of the Confederacy preserve and display flags, uniforms, swords, and other Civil War memorabilia. *188 Meeting St., Market area, tel. 843/723–1541, $5. Mon.–Sat. 10–4, Sun. 1–4.*

❻ OLD CITADEL BUILDING. Built in 1822 to house state troops and arms, this fortresslike building—now the Embassy Suites Historic Charleston—faces Marion Square. This is where the Carolina Military College—the Citadel—had its start. (The Citadel is now on the Ashley River.) *Upper King.*

⓬ OLD CITY MARKET. A series of low sheds that once housed produce and fish markets, this area is often called the Slave Market, although Charlestonians dispute that slaves ever were sold there. It now has restaurants, shops, gimcracks and gewgaws for children, vegetable-and-fruit vendors, and local "basket ladies" weaving and selling sweet-grass, pine-straw, and palmetto-leaf baskets—a craft passed down through generations from their West African ancestors. *Market St. between Meeting and E. Bay Sts., Market area. Daily 9–sunset, hrs may vary.*

⑱ OLD POWDER MAGAZINE. This structure was built in 1713 and used during the Revolutionary War. It is now a museum with costumes, armor, and other artifacts from 18th-century Charleston, plus a fascinating audiovisual tour. 79 Cumberland St., Market area, tel. 843/805-6730, www.historiccharleston.org. Free. Apr.–Oct., Mon.–Sat. 10–5, Sun. 2–5.

⑭ ST. JOHN'S LUTHERAN CHURCH. This Greek Revival church was built in 1817 for a congregation that was established in 1742. Notice the fine craftsmanship in the delicate wrought-iron gates and fence. Musicians may be interested in the 1823 Thomas Hall organ case. 5 Clifford St., Market area, tel. 843/723-2426, www.stjohns-lutheran.org. Weekdays 9:30–3:30.

⑩ ST. MARY'S CATHOLIC CHURCH. Established in 1839, this pretty white-pillared church is the earliest Roman Catholic church in the Carolinas and Georgia. Beautiful stained glass, wall paintings, and an enchanting cemetery tucked between stone walls are highlights. 89 Hasell St., Market area, tel. 843/722-7696. By appointment.

⑲ ST. PHILIP'S EPISCOPAL CHURCH. The graceful late-Georgian church is the second on its site; the congregation's first building burned down in 1838. You find the burial places of Charlestonians in the graveyard on the church side of the street; "foreigners" (including John C. Calhoun, who was from the faraway location of Abbeville, South Carolina) lie in the graveyard on the other side. 146 Church St., Market area, tel. 843/722-7734. By appointment.

SLAVE MART MUSEUM. Here—at a spot where slaves were once bought and sold—exhibits highlight the African-American experience in Charleston, from slavery to emancipation and reconstruction, and, finally, to the civil rights movement. 6 Chalmers St., Market area. Mon.–Sat. 9–5.

⑮ UNITARIAN CHURCH. Completed in 1787, this church was remodeled in the mid-19th century using plans inspired by the

Chapel of Henry VII in Westminster Abbey. The Gothic fan-tracery ceiling was added during that renovation. An entrance to the church grounds is on 161½–163 King Street. The secluded and romantically overgrown graveyard invites contemplation. 8 *Archdale St., Market area, tel. 843/723–4617. Weekdays 8:30–2:30. Sept.–May, 11 AM service.*

❶ VISITOR INFORMATION CENTER. The center gives a fine introduction to the city and sells tickets for shuttle services. Garage parking is $1 per hour; the first hour is free if you purchase a $2 shuttle pass. Take time to see *Forever Charleston*, an insightful 20-minute film. For $32.95 you can also buy a Charleston Heritage Passport, good for admission at Gibbes Museum of Art, Nathaniel Russell House, Edmondston-Alston House, Aiken-Rhett House, Drayton Hall, and Middleton Place. *375 Meeting St., Upper King, tel. 843/853–8000 or 800/868–8118. www.charlestoncvb.com. Film $2.50. Mar.–Oct., daily 8:30–5:30; Nov.–Feb., daily 8:30–5; shows daily 9–5 on the ½ hr.*

㉒ WATERFRONT PARK. A sprinkle from the park's interactive fountain will refresh you on hot summer days. Here you'll also find swings, a fishing pier, picnic tables, and gardens overlooking Charleston Harbor. It's at the foot of Vendue Range, along the east side of Charleston Harbor. *Market area, tel. 843/724–7321. Free. Daily 6 AM–midnight.*

NEED A BREAK? With a great view of the harbor and Waterfront Park, the **ROOFTOP LOUNGE AT VENDUE INN** (19 Vendue Range, Market area, tel. 843/577–7970 or 800/845–7900) serves drinks and appetizers alfresco.

THE BATTERY AND SOUTH OF BROAD

Along the Battery, on the point of a narrow peninsula bounded by the Ashley and Cooper rivers, handsome mansions surrounded by gardens face the harbor. Their distinctive look is reminiscent of the West Indies: before coming to the Carolinas in the late 17th century, many early British colonists had first settled on Barbados and other Caribbean isles, where they'd built houses with high ceilings and broad piazzas at each level to catch the sea breezes. In Charleston they adapted these designs. One type—narrow two- to four-story "single houses" built at right angles to the street—emerged partly because buildings were taxed according to the length of their frontage.

Heavily residential, the area south of Broad Street has many beautiful private homes, almost all of which have a plaque with a short written description of the home's history. You might get a peek at tucked-away English-style gardens, too. An open gate in Charleston once signified that all were welcome to venture inside for a closer look at the owner's garden. Open gates are rare today, but keep an eye out, as you never know when you'll get lucky.

Numbers in the text correspond to numbers in the margin and on the Charleston map.

A Good Walk

Start at the top of Broad Street at the **OLD EXCHANGE BUILDING/PROVOST DUNGEON** ㉓, which held prisoners during the American Revolution. Two blocks down Broad Street are the Four Corners of Law, including **CITY HALL** ㉔, with some historical displays and portraits, and **ST. MICHAEL'S EPISCOPAL CHURCH** ㉕, the city's oldest surviving church. In the famously affluent South of Broad neighborhood are several of the city's lavish house museums. The **HEYWARD-WASHINGTON HOUSE** ㉖ is a block south of Broad Street on Church Street. Next to it is picturesque Cabbage Row, the inspiration for Catfish Row in *Porgy and Bess*. The **NATHANIEL RUSSELL HOUSE** ㉗ and the **CALHOUN MANSION** ㉘ are on Meeting Street, are about two blocks apart on Meeting Street. Around the corner is the **EDMONDSTON-ALSTON HOUSE** ㉙, overlooking

Charleston's famous **BATTERY** ㉚ and Charleston Harbor. A park bench in the shade of **WHITE POINT GARDENS** ㉛, so named because of the bleached whiteness of oyster shells left here by Native Americans, is a splendid spot for a rest. From here go north along the Cooper River by shuttle, car, or rickshaw to the **SOUTH CAROLINA AQUARIUM** ㉜. Next door, at the Fort Sumter Visitor Education Center, at Liberty Square, you can catch the ferry for a harbor ride to **FORT SUMTER NATIONAL MONUMENT** ㉝.

TIMING

Plan to spend from two to four hours doing this walk, depending on your pace and which buildings you visit. A trip to the aquarium can add two or so hours, as will a trip to Fort Sumter; you may wish to split the trip into two half-days.

What to See

㉚ **THE BATTERY.** This sea wall and promenade has sweeping views of Charleston Harbor. *Murray Blvd., South of Broad.*

㉘ **CALHOUN MANSION.** Opulent by Charleston standards, this is a no-holds-barred example of Victorian taste. Built in 1876, this 24,000-square-ft mansion is full of ornate plasterwork and fine wood moldings and has a 75-ft dome ceiling. *16 Meeting St., South of Broad, tel. 843/722–8205. $15. Feb.–Dec., Wed.–Sun. 10–4.*

㉔ **CITY HALL.** The intersection of Meeting and Broad streets is known as the Four Corners of Law, representing the laws of nation, state, city, and church. On the northeast corner is the graceful City Hall, dating from 1801. The second-floor council chambers has historical displays and portraits, including John Trumbull's 1791 satirical portrait of George Washington and Samuel F. B. Morse's likeness of James Monroe. *80 Broad St., South of Broad, tel. 843/577–6970 or 843/724–3799. Free. Weekdays 10–5.*

OFF THE BEATEN PATH **COLONIAL LAKE** – Joggers, walkers, and folks looking for a tranquil city spot flock to this small man-made lake circled by a wide sidewalk, trees, and benches. In the late 19th century Colonial Common, as it was called at the time, was a popular gathering place for Victorian Charleston. Today it is surrounded by stately Victorian buildings. *Ashley and Rutledge Aves. to the east and west, Broad and Beaufain Sts. to the north and south, South of Broad, tel. 843/724–7327.*

㉙ **EDMONDSTON-ALSTON HOUSE.** With commanding views of Charleston Harbor, this imposing home was built in 1825 in late-federal style and transformed into a Greek Revival structure during the 1840s. It is tastefully furnished with antiques, portraits, Piranesi prints, silver, and fine china. *21 E. Battery, South of Broad, tel. 843/722–7171, www.middletonplace.org. $8; combination ticket with Middleton Place $27. Tues.–Sat. 10–4:30, Sun.–Mon. 1:30–4:30.*

★ ☞ ㉝ **FORT SUMTER NATIONAL MONUMENT.** It was here, on a man-made island in Charleston Harbor, that Confederate forces fired the first shot of the Civil War, on April 12, 1861. After a 34-hour bombardment Union forces surrendered and Confederate troops occupied Sumter, which became a symbol of Southern resistance. The Confederacy held the fort, despite almost continual bombardment, for nearly four years, and when it was finally evacuated, it was a heap of rubble. Today National Park Service rangers conduct free guided tours of the restored structure, which includes a free **museum** (tel. 843/883–3123) with historical displays. The fort is accessible only by boat; ferries depart from Patriots Point or the **Fort Sumter Visitor Center at Liberty Square,** next to the South Carolina Aquarium, which contains exhibits on the introduction of the war. *340 Concord St., Upper King, tel. 843/727–4739 for visitor center; 843/881–7337 or 800/789–3678 for Fort Sumter Tours Inc., www.nps.gov/fosu. Museum free, ferry fare $11. Tours Apr.–early Sept., 9:30, noon, 2:30, and 4; early Sept.–Mar., 9:30, noon, and 2:30.*

26 HEYWARD-WASHINGTON HOUSE. Built in 1772 by rice king Daniel Heyward, this home was the backdrop for DuBose Heyward's book *Porgy*, which was the basis for the beloved folk opera *Porgy and Bess*. The neighborhood, known as Cabbage Row, is central to Charleston's African-American history. President George Washington stayed in the house during his 1791 visit. It is full of fine period furnishings by such local craftsmen as Thomas Elfe, and its restored 18th-century kitchen is the only one in Charleston open to visitors. *87 Church St., South of Broad, tel. 843/722–0354, www.charlestonmuseum.com. $8; museum and houses $18; 2 of 3 sights $12. Mon.–Sat. 10–5, Sun. 1–5.*

★ **27 NATHANIEL RUSSELL HOUSE.** One of the nation's finest examples of Adam-style architecture, the Nathaniel Russell House was built in 1808. The interior is distinguished by its ornate detailing, its lavish period furnishings, and the "flying" circular staircase that spirals three stories with no apparent support. *51 Meeting St., South of Broad, tel. 843/724–8481, www.historiccharleston.org. $7, combination ticket with Aiken-Rhett House $12. Mon.–Sat. 10–5, Sun. 2–5.*

23 OLD EXCHANGE BUILDING/PROVOST DUNGEON. Originally a customs house, this building was used by the British to house prisoners during the Revolutionary War. Today a tableau of lifelike mannequins recalls this era. *122 E. Bay St., South of Broad, tel. 843/727–2165, www.oldexchange.com. $6. Daily 9–5.*

25 ST. MICHAEL'S EPISCOPAL CHURCH. Modeled after London's St. Martin-in-the-Fields and completed in 1761, this is Charleston's oldest surviving church. Its steeple clock and bells were imported from England in 1764. *14 St. Michael's Alley, South of Broad, tel. 843/723–0603, www.stmichaelschurch.net. Weekdays 9–5, Sat. 9–noon.*

NEED A BREAK? On your way down Broad Street toward Church Street, duck into the dark-paneled, tin-ceiling **BLIND TIGER PUB** (38 Broad St., South of Broad, tel. 843/577–0088) for a drink or beer on the patio out back, or a meal from the Four Corners Cafe next door.

★ ◐ ㉜ **SOUTH CAROLINA AQUARIUM.** The 322,000-gallon Great Ocean Tank has the tallest aquarium window in North America. Exhibits display more than 10,000 living organisms, representing more than 500 species. You travel through the five major regions of the Southeast Appalachian Watershed as found in South Carolina: the Blue Ridge Mountains, the Piedmont, the coastal plain, the coast, and the ocean. The little ones can pet stingrays at one touch tank and horseshoe crabs and conchs at another. *3250 Concord St., Upper King, tel. 843/720–1990 or 800/722–6455, www. scaquarium.org. $14. July–Aug., daily 9–7; Mar.–June and Sept.–Oct., daily 9–5; Nov.–Feb., daily 10–5.*

◐ ㉛ **WHITE POINT GARDENS.** Pirates once hung from gallows here; now this park, with a gazebo, Charleston benches, and views of the harbor and Fort Sumter, is the number one marriage site in the city. Children love to climb on the cannon and cannonball replicas. *Murray Blvd. and E. Battery, South of Broad, tel. 843/724–7327. Weekdays 9–5, Sat. 9–noon.*

MOUNT PLEASANT AND VICINITY

East of Charleston across the Cooper River Bridge, via U.S. 17N, is the town of Mount Pleasant, named not for a mountain or a hill but for a plantation in England from which some of the area's settlers hailed. In its Old Village neighborhood are antebellum homes and a sleepy, old-time town center that has a drugstore with an old-fashioned soda fountain. Along Shem Creek, where the local fishing fleet brings in the daily catch, are several seafood restaurants. Other attractions in the area are museums, plantations, and, farther north, the Cape Romain National Wildlife Refuge.

A Good Tour

There's enough adventure here to stretch over a number of days, especially if you're a war history buff. On the first day you might drive to **PATRIOTS POINT,** veering right from the Cooper River

Bridge onto Coleman Boulevard in the direction of Sullivan's Island and the Isle of Palms. Later, continue along Coleman Boulevard and, just after crossing the boat-lined docks and restaurants at Shem Creek, turn right at Whilden Street for a drive through the Old Village. Returning to Coleman Boulevard, you'll pass the Common, a cluster of shops on your left. Stop here for the **MUSEUM ON THE COMMON**, featuring the *Hurricane Hugo Revisited* exhibit. Follow the signs to **FORT MOULTRIE**. Spend the rest of the day relaxing on the beach or bicycling through Sullivan's Island, a residential community of early 20th-century beach houses, or the Isle of Palms, which has a pavilion and more abundant parking.

On another day, drive out U.S. 17N 8 mi to **BOONE HALL PLANTATION** and its famous Avenue of Oaks, stopping at nearby **CHARLES PINCKNEY NATIONAL HISTORIC SITE**, with interpretations of African-American life on the plantation. Bring a picnic and rent bikes at **PALMETTO ISLANDS COUNTY PARK**, across Boone Hall Creek from the plantation; you'll need a swimsuit for Splash Island, a mini–water park. Another option is a ferry ride and visit to Bull Island, part of the **CAPE ROMAIN NATIONAL WILDLIFE REFUGE**, one of the nation's most pristine wildlife areas. The Sewee Visitor & Environmental Education Center (on U.S. 17, 35 mi north of Charleston) has information and exhibits on the refuge as well as live birds of prey, red wolves, and trails.

TIMING
You need three days to see all the attractions here; if you have one day or less, choose a few based on your interests.

What to See

★ **BOONE HALL PLANTATION.** This plantation is approached along one of the South's most majestic avenues of oaks, which was the model for the grounds of Tara in *Gone With the Wind*. You can tour the first floor of the classic columned mansion, which was built in 1935, incorporating woodwork and flooring from the original house. The primary attraction is the grounds, with formal azalea and camellia gardens, as well as the original slave quarters—the only "slave street" still intact in the Southeast—and the cotton-gin house used in the made-for-television movies *North and South* and *Queen*. *1235 Long Point Rd., off U.S. 17N, Mount Pleasant/East Cooper, tel. 843/884–4371. $12.50. Apr.–early Sept., Mon.–Sat. 8:30–6:30, Sun. 1–5; early Sept.–Mar., Mon.–Sat. 9–5, Sun. 1–4.*

NEED A BREAK? Driving north of Mount Pleasant along U.S. 17, you'll see **BASKET LADIES** at roadside stands. If you have the heart to bargain, you *may* be able to purchase the baskets at somewhat lower prices than in Charleston. But remember that you are buying a nearly lost art, and sweet grass is no longer plentiful in the wild.

CAPE ROMAIN NATIONAL WILDLIFE REFUGE. A grouping of barrier islands and salt marshes, this 60,000-acre refuge is one of the most outstanding in the country. At the **Sewee Visitor & Environmental Education Center** you can view exhibits about the refuge and arrange to take a ferry to Bull Island for a day visit. The island is a nearly untouched wilderness; the beach here, strewn with bleached driftwood, is nicknamed Bone Beach. *5821 U.S. 17N, Awendaw, tel. 843/928–3368. Free. Daily 9–5.*

CHARLES PINCKNEY NATIONAL HISTORIC SITE. Across the street from Boone Hall, this is the only protected remnant of the country estate of Charles Pinckney, drafter and signer of the Constitution. A self-guided tour explores many fascinating interpretations of African-American life, including the plantation owner–slave relationship. You can also tour an 1820s tidewater cottage. *1254 Long Point Rd., off U.S. 17N, Mount Pleasant/East Cooper, tel. 843/881–5516, fax 843/881–7070, www. nps.gov/chpi. Free. Daily 9–5.*

🏛 **FORT MOULTRIE.** Here Colonel William Moultrie's South Carolinians repelled a British assault in one of the first Patriot victories of the Revolutionary War. Completed in 1809, this is the third fort on this site at **Sullivan's Island,** which you'll reach on Route 703 off U.S. 17N (8 mi southeast of Charleston). A 20-minute film tells the history of the fort. *W. Middle St., Mount Pleasant/East Cooper Sullivan's Island, tel. 843/883–3123. $2. Daily 9–5.*

🏛 **MUSEUM ON THE COMMON.** This small museum has an outdoor maritime museum and a Hurricane Hugo exhibit prepared by the South Carolina State Museum; it shows the 1989 storm damage through video and photos. *217 Lucas St., Mount Pleasant/East Cooper, Shem Creek Village, Mount Pleasant, tel. 843/849–9000. Free. Mon.–Sat. 10–4.*

🏛 **PALMETTO ISLANDS COUNTY PARK.** You'll find a Big Toy playground, 2-acre pond, paved trails, an observation tower, marsh boardwalks, and a "water island" at this park across Boone Hall Creek from Boone Hall Plantation. Bicycles and paddleboats can be rented in season. *Long Point Rd. (½ mi past Boone Hall Plantation), Mount Pleasant/East Cooper, tel. 843/884–0832. $2. Apr. and Sept.–Oct., daily 9–6; May–Aug., daily 9–7; Nov.–Feb., daily 10–5; Mar., daily 10–6.*

★ 🏛 **PATRIOTS POINT.** Tours are available on all vessels here at the world's largest naval and maritime museum, which now houses the Medal of Honor Society. Berthed here are the aircraft carrier USS *Yorktown,* the World War II submarine USS *Clamagore,* the destroyer USS *Laffey,* the nuclear merchant ship *Savannah,* and the Coast Guard cutter *Ingham,* responsible for sinking a U-boat during World War II. The film *The Fighting Lady* is shown regularly aboard the *Yorktown,* and there is a Vietnam exhibit. *Foot of Cooper River Bridge, Mount Pleasant/East Cooper, tel. 843/884–2727, www.state.sc.us/patpt. $11. Early Sept.–Mar., daily 9–6:30; Apr.–early Sept., daily 9–7:30.*

WEST OF THE ASHLEY RIVER

A Good Tour

The sights covered here are each a few miles apart along Ashley River Road, Route 61, which begins a few miles northwest of downtown Charleston over the Ashley River Bridge. Still, you'll need time to see them all. One day you could spend a few hours exploring **CHARLES TOWNE LANDING STATE PARK,** veering off Route 61 onto Old Towne Road (Route 171); then finish your day at **MIDDLETON GARDENS.** Another day you might tour the majestic simplicity of **DRAYTON HALL** before continuing on to **MAGNOLIA PLANTATION AND GARDENS** and all their splendor.

TIMING

Nature and garden enthusiasts can easily spend a full day at Magnolia Gardens, Middleton Gardens, or Charles Towne Landing State Park, so budget your time accordingly. Spring is a peak time for the gardens, although they are lovely throughout the year.

What to See

★ ⓒ **CHARLES TOWNE LANDING STATE PARK.** Commemorating the site of the original 1670 Charleston settlement, this park on Route 171 has a reconstructed village and fortifications, English park gardens with bicycle trails and walkways, and a replica 17th-century vessel moored in the creek. In the animal park native species roam freely—among them alligators, bison, pumas, bears, and wolves. Bicycle and kayak rentals and cassette and tram tours are available. The park has begun a $5 million renovation that includes a comprehensive archaeological dig and a new visitor center–museum. *1500 Old Towne Rd., West Ashley, tel. 843/852–4200, www.southcarolinaparks.com. $5. Late May–early Sept., daily 9–6; early Sept.–late May, daily 9–5.*

★ **DRAYTON HALL.** Considered the nation's finest example of unspoiled Georgian-Palladian architecture, this mansion is the only plantation house on the Ashley River to have survived the Civil War. A National Historic Landmark, built between 1738 and 1742, it is an invaluable lesson in history as well as in architecture. Drayton Hall has been left unfurnished to highlight the original plaster moldings, opulent hand-carved woodwork, and other ornamental details. Connections, an African-American focus presentation offered before the tour, is fascinating. You will learn about the conditions under which slaves were brought from Africa and can view copies of documents recording the buying and selling of local plantation slaves. *3380 Ashley River Rd., 13 mi north of Charleston, West Ashley, tel. 843/766–0188, www.draytonhall.org. $12. Guided tours Mar.–Oct., daily 10–4; Nov.–Feb., daily 10–3.*

☙ **MAGNOLIA PLANTATION AND GARDENS.** The 50-acre informal garden, begun in 1685, has a huge collection of azaleas and camellias. A tram will take you for an overall tour with three stops. You can canoe through the 125-acre Waterfowl Refuge, explore the 30-acre **Audubon Swamp Garden** along boardwalks and bridges, or walk or bicycle more than 500 acres of wildlife trails. Tours of the manor house, built during Reconstruction, depict plantation life. The grounds also hold a petting zoo and a miniature-horse ranch. *3550 Ashley River Rd., just north of Drayton Hall, West Ashley, tel. 843/571–1266 or 800/367–3517, www.magnoliaplantation.com. $12; house tour $7 extra; nature tram $6 extra; nature boat tour $5 extra; swamp garden $6; canoe and bike rentals. Daily 8–5:30.*

★ ☙ **MIDDLETON PLACE.** The nation's oldest landscaped gardens, dating from 1741, are magnificently ablaze with camellias, magnolias, azaleas, roses, and flowers of all seasons planted in floral *allées* and terraced lawns and around ornamental lakes. Much of the mansion was destroyed during the Civil War, but the south wing has been restored and houses impressive collections of silver, furniture, paintings, and historic documents. In the stable yard craftspeople use authentic tools and equipment to demonstrate spinning, blacksmithing, and other domestic skills from the plantation era. Farm animals, peacocks, and other creatures roam freely. The Middleton Place restaurant serves Lowcountry specialties for lunch daily; a gift shop carries local arts, crafts, and souvenirs. Also on the grounds is a modern Danish-style inn (access to the gardens is included in the room price) with floor-to-ceiling windows dramatizing views of the Ashley River; here you can sign up for kayaking and biking tours. *Ashley River Rd. (4 mi north of Magnolia Plantation), West Ashley, tel. 843/556-6020 or 800/782-3608, www.middletonplace.org. $15; house tours $8 extra. Daily 9–5; house tours Tues.–Sun. 10–4:30, Mon. 1:30–4:30.*

OFF THE BEATEN PATH **AMERICAN CLASSIC TEA PLANTATION** – On a small rural island about 20 mi southwest of Charleston on Route 700 is the country's only commercial tea plantation. Tours run from May through October and cover tea history, harvesting, and production and include a discussion with the plantation's official tea taster. The tour ends with tea and cookies. *6617 Maybank Hwy., Wadmalaw Island, tel. 800/443-5987. Free. May–Oct., 1st Sat. each month 10–1:30.*

🕐 **ANGEL OAK** – This magnificent live oak has a massive canopy that creates 17,000 square ft of shade. Long a favorite with local children because of its bending branches that slope gently, armlike to the ground, Angel Oak is believed to be more than 1,400 years old. It's about 12 mi southwest of Charleston off Route 700. *3688 Angel Oak Rd., Johns Island, tel. 843/559-3496. Free. Daily 9–4:45.*

🕐 **CAW CAW INTERPRETIVE CENTER** – Once part of a 1700s rice plantation, this 650-acre cypress swamp park has 8 mi of historical and interpretive trails that include a 1,200-ft marsh boardwalk, informative and well-executed exhibits on rice cultivation, Gullah storytelling, and African-American music and craft demonstrations, and an in-depth documentation of the vital role slaves played in the rice fields. It's about 15 mi west of Charleston on U.S. 17. *5200 Savannah Hwy., Ravenel, tel. 843/889–8898, www.ccprc.com/cawcaw.htm. $4. Nov.–Feb., Tues.–Sun. 9–5; Mar.–Apr. and Sept.–Oct., Tues.–Sun. 9–6; May–Aug., Tues.–Sun. 8–7.*

EATING OUT

She-crab soup, sautéed shrimp and grits, variations on pecan pie, and other Lowcountry specialties are served all over the Charleston area—as are creative contemporary dishes crafted by local chefs. Outstanding eateries, from seafood houses to elegant French restaurants, make Charleston a favorite for gastronomes. Trendy Mount Pleasant, across the East Cooper Bridge, has a number of good restaurants.

CATEGORY	COST*
$$$$	over $25
$$$	$17–$25
$$	$10–$17
$	under $10

*per person for a main course at dinner

Contemporary

$$$–$$$$ **CIRCA 1886.** If you've got an occasion for champagne cocktails and foie gras, celebrate at this formal, conducive-to-conversation dining room in a carriage house behind the Wentworth Mansion. Grilled antelope loin with sweet-potato spoon bread and chocolate Bailey's Irish cream soufflé are the signature dishes. *149 Wentworth St., Market area, tel. 843/853–7828. AE, D, DC, MC, V. No lunch.*

$$$–$$$$ **MCCRADY'S.** This elegant restaurant, in a 1778 tavern, has locals ★ raving over its potato gnocchi, tuna tartare, grouper with a creamy leek sauce and truffle oil, herb-marinated rack of lamb with mint

drizzle, and bitter-chocolate bread pudding. The dining room is elegant and somewhat formal; the long bar has cozy booths. 2 Unity Alley, Market area, tel. 843/577–0025. AE, MC, V. No lunch.

\$\$\$–\$\$\$\$ PENINSULA GRILL. ★ Surrounded by walls covered in olive-green velvet, black-iron chandeliers, and 18th-century-style portraits, diners at this busy spot in the Planters Inn can feast on such delights as lobster citron, rabbit loin wrapped in veal bacon with tapenade linguine and mustard vinaigrette, and New Zealand benne-seed-encrusted rack of lamb with wild mushroom potatoes and coconut-mint pesto. 112 N. Market St., Market area, tel. 843/723–0700. AE, D, DC, MC, V. No lunch. Jackets essential.

\$\$\$ CYPRESS. From the owners of Magnolias and Blossom Cafe comes this sleek restaurant in a renovated 1834 brick-wall building, now very groovy with rust-color leather booths, a ceiling with circular lights that change color, and an entire "wine wall" of 4,000 bottles under glass. Here you'll find not only wonderful vino, but also a fabulous arugula salad with apples, Gorgonzola and pecans; green tea-smoked duck; and hickory-grilled fillet with a house-made Boursin cheese and Madeira sauce. If you've forgotten the jacket, dine upstairs. 167 E. Bay St., Market area, tel. 843/727–0111. AE, D, DC, MC, V. No lunch.

\$\$ SERMET'S CORNER. Colorful, bold artwork by chef Sermet Aslan decorates the walls of this lively eatery. The Mediterranean-influenced menu has panini (grilled Italian sandwiches), seafood, and flavorful pastas. The poached pear salad and lavender pork are favorites. 276 King St., Market area, tel. 843/853–7775. AE, MC, V.

French

\$\$\$\$ ROBERT'S OF CHARLESTON. A classically trained singer and chef, Robert offers a special experience: four rich, generously portioned courses (scallop mousse with lobster sauce, duckling with grilled vegetables, roast tenderloin with bordelaise sauce,

charleston dining and lodging

KEY

🏨 hotels

① restaurants

DINING

Alice's Fine Foods, 5
Anson, 17
Boathouse Rest., 4
Boulevard Diner, 3
Carolina's, 25
Charleston Grill, 14
Circa 1886, 11
Cypress, 20
Doe's Pita Plus, 9
Elliott's on the Square, 6
Fulton Five, 12
Gaulart and Maliclet Café, 24
High Cotton, 18
Hominy Grill, 7
Il Cortile del Re, 13
J. Bistro, 2

Magnolias, 21
McCrady's, 23
Peninsula Grill, 16
Robert's of Charleston, 22
Sermet's Corner, 10
Slightly North of Broad, 19
Sticky Fingers, 15
39 Rue de Jean Bar Cafe, 8
The Wreck, 1

LODGING

Ansonborough Inn, 11
Best Western King Charles Inn, 12
Cannonboro Inn and Ashley Inn, 9
Charleston Pl., 15

Doubletree Guest Suites Historic Charleston, 17
1837 Bed and Breakfast and Tea Room, 13
Elliott House Inn, 21
Embassy Suites Historic Charleston, 6
Guilds Inn, 3
Hampton Inn—Charleston North, 1
Hampton Inn–Historic District, 5
Harbor View Inn, 19
Hayne House, 23
Holiday Inn Charleston/ Mt. Pleasant, 2

Holiday Inn Historic District, 7
John Rutledge House Inn, 22
Meeting Street Inn, 18
Mills House Hotel, 24
Phoebe Pember House, 10
Planters Inn, 16
Red Roof Inn, 4
Two Meeting St., 25
Vendue Inn, 20
Wentworth Mansion, 14
Westin Francis Marion Hotel, 8

and dessert) with lovely wines, impeccable service, and the best of Broadway tunes in a warm, intimate dining room. *182 E. Bay St., Market area, tel. 843/577–7565. MC, V. Closed Sun.–Wed. No lunch.*

$$–$$$ **39 RUE DE JEAN BAR CAFE.** In classy, traditional French style— gleaming wood, white-papered tables, and booths—the trendy set dines late (until 1 AM, except Sunday) on wonderful mussels, steak frites, scallops St. Jacques, and even sushi. It's noisy and happening, but there's a quiet back room. *39 John St., Upper King, tel. 843/722–8881. AE, D, DC, MC, V. No lunch weekends.*

$–$$ **GAULART AND MALICLET CAFÉ.** This casual, chic eatery serves Continental dishes—breads and pastries, soups, salads, sandwiches, and specials such as seafood Normandy and chicken sesame. *98 Broad St., South of Broad, tel. 843/577–9797. AE, D, MC, V. Closed Sun. No dinner Mon.*

Italian

$$$–$$$$ **FULTON FIVE.** There are just 15 tables in this romantic restaurant on a side road off King Street. The chartreuse walls and antique brass accents provide the perfect environment for savoring northern Italian specialties, such as risotto, lemon sherbet with Campari, and antipasto Spoleto (mozzarella and prosciutto wrapped in a romaine lettuce leaf and drizzled with olive oil and diced tomatoes). *5 Fulton St., Market area, tel. 843/853–5555. AE, DC, MC, V. Closed Sun. and late Aug.–1st wk Sept. No lunch.*

$$–$$$ **IL CORTILE DEL RE.** Great wines, hearty soups and pastas, and lovely cheeses and breads make it feel just like Tuscany here. Tucked off King Street behind a women's clothing shop, this hard-to-find spot has a cozy back room and a romantic courtyard with a crumbling brick wall. *193 King St., Market area, tel. 843/853–1888. AE, DC, MC, V. Closed Sun.–Mon. No lunch Thurs.–Sat.*

Lowcountry

$$–$$$$ **SLIGHTLY NORTH OF BROAD.** This high-ceiling former warehouse with brick-and-stucco walls has several seats looking directly into the exposed kitchen (great for single diners). Chef Frank Lee's inventive dishes include grilled barbecued tuna with fried oysters and sautéed squab with coriander. You can order most items as either a small plate or a main course. The extensive wine list is moderately priced. A sister restaurant, **Slightly Up the Creek** (130 Mill St., Mt. Pleasant, tel. 843/884–5005; no lunch; brunch only on Sun.), at Shem Creek in Mount Pleasant, has waterfront views and more seafood dishes. *192 E. Bay St., Market area, tel. 843/723–3424. Reservations not accepted for lunch. AE, D, DC, MC, V. No lunch weekends.*

$$–$$$ **CAROLINA'S.** This lively, casual bistro, styled in black and white, with terra-cotta tiles and 1920s French posters, has long been a favorite. Fans return for the "appeteasers" such as Crowder pea cakes (made with Crowder peas, spices, egg, and bread crumbs) and fried calamari, plus smoked baby-back ribs and pasta with crawfish and tasso. Dinner entrées are selections from the grill, including pork tenderloin with Jamaican seasoning and salmon with cilantro, ginger, and lime butter. *10 Exchange St., South of Broad, tel. 843/724–3800. Reservations essential. D, MC, V. No lunch.*

Lowcountry/Southern

$$$–$$$$ **ANSON.** After an afternoon of strolling through the Old City Market, you can walk up Anson Street to this softly lighted, gilt-trimmed dining room. Framed by about a dozen French windows, Anson's has elegant booths anchored by marble-top tables. New South specialties include shrimp and grits, fried corn-bread oysters, and barbecued grouper. The she-crab soup is some of the best around. *12 Anson St., Market area, tel. 843/577–0551. AE, D, DC, MC, V. No lunch.*

$$$–$$$$ **CHARLESTON GRILL.** Its clubby chairs and dark paneling create
★ a comfortably elegant venue for chef Bob Waggoner's famously
fabulous new South cuisine. Dishes include lump crab cake over
yellow tomato coulis, venison tenderloin with caramelized
mushrooms and truffle potatoes, zucchini blossoms stuffed with
lobster mousse, and beef medallions over garlic grits. Many
nights there's live jazz. *224 King St., Charleston Place Hotel, Market
area, tel. 843/577–4522. AE, D, DC, MC, V.*

$$$–$$$$ **HIGH COTTON.** Feast on spit-roasted and grilled meats and fish
in this elegant and airy, brick-walled eatery studded with palm
trees. Weeknight specials are great deals; at the popular bar
there is live jazz. The chocolate soufflé with blackberry sauce and
the praline soufflé are fabulous. *199 E. Bay St., Market area, tel. 843/
724–3815. AE, D, DC, MC, V. No lunch weekdays.*

$$$–$$$$ **MAGNOLIAS.** Locals love this popular place, in an 1823 warehouse,
★ with a magnolia theme evident in its vivid paintings, etched glass,
wrought iron, and candlesticks. The uptown down-South cuisine
shines with its specialties: egg roll stuffed with chicken and collard
greens with a spicy mustard sauce and sweet pepper purée.
Equally innovative appetizers include seared yellow-grits cakes
with tasso gravy, yellow corn relish, and sautéed greens. You may
also want to try the **Blossom Café** (171 E. Bay St., Market area,
tel. 843/722–9200), owned by the same people but with a more
Continental menu, including pizzas cooked in a wood-burning
oven, pastas, and fish. *185 E. Bay St., Market area, tel. 843/577–7771.
Reservations essential. AE, DC, MC, V.*

$$–$$$ **ELLIOTT'S ON THE SQUARE.** Come to this bright and cheerful
restaurant if you have a hankering for Southern Sunday-dinner-
style entrées for lunch and dinner, including black-eyed pea
cakes, fried chicken, barbecued salmon over grits, and butter
pound cake. The food may be down-home, but the service is not.
*387 King St., Francis Marion Hotel, Upper King, tel. 843/724–8888. AE,
D, DC, MC, V.*

$$–$$$ J. BISTRO. Funky steel cutouts liven up the outside and inside walls, and the lighting is whimsical—hanging low over tables lined up against a banquette. A varied list of appetizers and small plates makes this a great place to graze. Choose from such innovations as steamed lobster wontons, grouper with a champagne-crabmeat cream sauce, and pecan-crusted catfish over grits. The lamb chops are superb. It's about 7 to 10 mi from town. *819 Coleman Blvd., Mount Pleasant/East Cooper, tel. 843/971–7778. Reservations essential. AE, MC, V. Closed Mon. No dinner Sun. No lunch.*

$–$$$ HOMINY GRILL. Locals lunch and brunch at this breezy café-style restaurant. Although a bit off the beaten path (a few blocks east of King Street), it's worth a special trip. The young chef's Southern upbringing is evident in everything from the vegetable plate (collards, squash casserole, black-eyed pea cakes with guacamole, and mushroom hominy) to the pimiento cheese sandwich and the turkey club with homemade french fries. The avocado and *wehani* rice (a clay-colored, aromatic variety of brown rice) salad with grilled vegetables is a refreshing don't-miss in summer. Leave room for the excellent buttermilk pie or bread pudding. *207 Rutledge Ave., Upper King, tel. 843/937–0930. AE, MC, V. No dinner Sun.*

$–$$$ STICKY FINGERS. Specializing in ribs six ways (Memphis style wet and dry, Texas style wet and dry, Carolina sweet, and Tennessee whiskey) and barbecue, this family-friendly restaurant has locations downtown and in Mount Pleasant and Summerville. Tuesday night is children's night, with supervised games and cartoons in a playroom. *235 Meeting St., Market area, tel. 843/853–7427 or 800/671–5966; 341 Johnnie Dodds Blvd., Mount Pleasant/East Cooper, tel. 843/856–9840; 1200 N. Main St., Summerville, tel. 843/875–7969. AE, DC, MC, V.*

$–$$ ALICE'S FINE FOODS. The food Southerners crave is here in its
★ original, beloved form: baked or fried chicken, ribs, fried fish, and other entrées come with a choice of three home-cooked vegetables and side dishes, including green beans, collard greens, red rice,

macaroni-and-cheese pie, okra and tomatoes, lima beans, rice and gravy, yams, and squash. The tone here is very casual, and the buffet is cafeteria-style. *468–470 King St., Upper King, tel. 843/ 853–9366. MC, V.*

$–$$ BOULEVARD DINER. There are no frills at this simple diner with booths and a counter and booths where the service is friendly and attentive, and the food is quite decent. Among the winners are: the daily variety of homemade veggies, the fried eggplant-and-blue-cheese sandwich, and the Cajun meatloaf and chili. *409 W. Coleman Blvd., Mount Pleasant/East Cooper, tel. 843/216–2611. MC, V. Closed Sun.*

Middle Eastern

$ DOE'S PITA PLUS. This is a favorite spot, at lunch in particular, among locals working downtown. Among the best-sellers: pitas stuffed with chicken salad, Greek salad, or avocado salad, pita chips, hummus, meat pies, tabbouleh. There's a simple grouping of small tables and chairs, as well as some outdoor seating. *334 E. Bay St., Market area, tel. 843/577–3179. AE. No dinner weekends.*

Seafood

$$–$$$ BOATHOUSE RESTAURANT. Large portions of fresh seafood at
★ reasonable prices make both locations of the Boathouse Restaurant wildly popular. The crab dip, fish specials, and lightly battered fried shrimp and oysters are irresistible. Entrées come with nice helpings of mashed potatoes, grits, collard greens, or blue-cheese coleslaw. The original Isle of Palms location is right on the water. *101 Palm Blvd., Isle of Palms, tel. 843/886–8000; 14 Chapel St., Upper King, tel. 843/577–7171. Reservations essential. AE, DC, MC, V.*

$$–$$$ THE WRECK. Dockside and full of wacky character, this spot serves up such traditional dishes as boiled peanuts, fried shrimp, shrimp pilaf, deviled crab, and oyster platters. They weren't kidding with the name—expect a shabby, candlelighted screened-in porch and small dining area. Nonetheless, it has a kind of seaside-joint charm. *106 Haddrell St., Mount Pleasant/East Cooper, tel. 843/884–0052. Reservations not accepted. No credit cards.*

SHOPPING

SHOPPING DISTRICTS

The Market is a complex of specialty shops and restaurants. Vendors sell beaded jewelry, hats, clothing, T-shirts, antique silver, and more in the open-air flea market called **OLD CITY MARKET** (E. Bay and Market Sts., Market area). You'll find locally made sweet-grass baskets here—and can even watch as they're crafted. **RAINBOW MARKET** (40 N. Market St., Market area) occupies two interconnected mid-19th-century buildings (don't miss the filled-to-the-hilt **Good Scents** in Rainbow Market, known for its perfume oils and lotions). **SHOPS AT CHARLESTON PLACE** (130 Market St., Market area) has Gucci, Cache, Limited Express, and Brookstone. **KING STREET** has some of Charleston's oldest and finest shops, including **Croghan's Jewel Box** (308 King St., Market area, tel. 843/723–3594), **Saks Fifth Avenue** (211 King St., Market area, tel. 843/853–9888), and the chichi **Christian Michi** (220 King St., Market area, tel. 843/723–0575), which carries elegant women's clothes, makeup, and housewares. From May until September a festive **FARMERS' MARKET** takes place Saturday mornings at Marion Square.

SPECIALTY SHOPS

Antiques

King Street is the center for antiques shopping. **BIRLANT & CO.** (191 King St., Market area, tel. 843/722–3842) presents fine 18th- and 19th-century English antiques, as well as the famous Charleston Battery bench, a small wood-slat bench with cast-iron sides. **PERIOD ANTIQUES** (194 King St., Market area, tel. 843/723–2724) has 18th- and 19th-century pieces. **PETTERSON ANTIQUES** (201 King St., Market area, tel. 843/723–5714) offers curious objets d'art, books, furniture, porcelain, and glass. **LIVINGSTON & SONS ANTIQUES,** dealers in 18th- and 19th-century English and Continental furniture, clocks, and bric-a-brac, has a large shop west of the Ashley River (2137 Savannah Hwy., West Ashley, tel. 843/556–6162) and a smaller one on King Street (163 King St., Market area, tel. 843/723–9697).

On James Island, a 10-minute drive from downtown, **CAROLOPOLIS ANTIQUES** (2000 Wappoo Dr., tel. 843/795–7724) has good bargains on country pieces, many of which are bought by downtown stores. On U.S. 17 in Mount Pleasant, **HUNGRYNECK MALL** (401 Johnnie Dodds Blvd., Mount Pleaant/East Cooper, tel. 843/849–1744) has more than 60 dealers hawking sterling silver, oak and mahogany furnishings, linens, and Civil War memorabilia. In Mount Pleasant, **PAGE'S THIEVES MARKET** (1460 Ben Sawyer Blvd., Mount Pleasant/East Cooper, tel. 843/884–9672) has furniture, glassware, and "junque."

Art and Crafts Galleries

The **BIRDS I VIEW GALLERY** (119A Church St., Market area, tel. 843/723–1276) sells bird paintings and prints by Anne Worsham Richardson. **CHARLESTON CRAFTS** (87 Hasell St., Market area, tel. 843/723–2938) has a fine selection of pottery, quilts, weavings, sculptures, and jewelry fashioned mostly by local artists. The **PINK HOUSE GALLERY** (17 Chalmers St., Market area, tel. 843/723–3608), in the oldest stone house in the city, has prints and paintings of traditional Charleston scenes by local artists. Be sure to go all the way to the third floor to get a look at the small, 17th-century living quarters. Prints of Elizabeth O'Neill Verner's pastels and etchings are on sale at **ELIZABETH O'NEILL VERNER STUDIO & GALLERY** (38 Tradd St.,

South of Broad, tel. 843/722–4246). The **MARTY WHALEY ADAMS GALLERY** (2 Queen St., Market area, tel. 843/853–8512) has original vivid watercolors and monotypes, plus prints and posters by this Charleston artist. At **NINA LIU AND FRIENDS** (24 State St., Market area, tel. 843/722–2724), you'll find contemporary art objects including handblown glass, pottery, jewelry, and photographs. Famous for his Lowcountry beach scenes, local watercolorist Steven Jordan displays his best at **STEVEN JORDAN GALLERY** (463 Coleman Blvd., Mount Pleasant/East Cooper, tel. 843/881–1644).

Books

ATLANTIC BOOKS (191 E. Bay St., Market area, tel. 843/723–7654; 310 King St., Upper King, tel. 843/723–4751), in two downtown locations, has historic, rare, and out-of-print books. The **PRESERVATION SOCIETY OF CHARLESTON** (King and Queen Sts., Market area, tel. 843/722–4630) carries books and tapes of historic and local interest, sweet-grass baskets, prints, and posters.

Gifts

Charleston's and London's own **BEN SILVER** (149 King St., Market area, tel. 843/577–4556), premier purveyor of blazer buttons, has more than 800 designs, including college and British regimental motifs. He also sells British neckties, embroidered polo shirts, and blazers. **BLINK** (62B Queen St., Market area, tel. 843/577–5688) has regionally and locally produced paintings, photos, pottery, jewelry, and garden art. **CHARLESTON COLLECTIONS** (Straw Market, Kiawah Island Resort, Johns Island, tel. 843/768–7487; 625 Skylark Dr., West Ashley, tel. 843/556–8911) has Charleston chimes, Rainbow Row prints, Charleston rice spoons and rice steamers, and more. **EAST BAY GALLERY** (280 W. Coleman Blvd., Mount Pleasant/East Cooper, tel. 843/216–8010) has jewelry, chess sets, chimes, and ceramics by local artists. The **SUGAR PLANTATION** (48 N. Market St., Market area, tel. 843/853–3924) has melt-in-your-mouth pralines, fudge, Charleston chews, and benne-seed wafers. You can find Charleston foods, including benne-seed wafers, pepper jelly, she-crab soup, and pickled okra, at area **PIGGLY WIGGLY** grocery stores (two locations: 1501 U.S. 17N, Mount Pleasant/East Cooper, tel. 843/881–7921; IOP Connector, Mount Pleasant/East Cooper, tel. 843/881–8939).

Period Reproductions

HISTORIC CHARLESTON REPRODUCTIONS (105 Broad St., South of Broad, tel. 843/723–8292) has superb replicas of Charleston furniture and accessories, all authorized by the Historic Charleston Foundation. Royalties from sales contribute to restoration projects. At the **OLD CHARLESTON JOGGLING BOARD CO.** (652 King St., Upper King, tel. 843/723–4331), these Lowcountry oddities (on which people bounce) can be purchased.

OUTDOOR ACTIVITIES AND SPORTS

BEACHES

The Charleston area's mild climate generally is conducive to swimming from April through October. This is definitely not a "swingles" area; all public and private beaches are family oriented, providing a choice of water sports, sunbathing, shelling, fishing, or quiet moonlight strolling. The **CHARLESTON COUNTY PARKS AND RECREATION COMMISSION** (tel. 843/762–2172) operates several public beach facilities.

BEACHWALKER PARK, on the west end of Kiawah Island (which is otherwise a private resort), has 300 ft of beach frontage, seasonal lifeguard service, rest rooms, outdoor showers, a picnic area, snack bar, and a 150-car parking lot. *Beachwalker Dr., Kiawah Island, tel. 843/768–2395. $5 per car (up to 8 passengers). June–Aug., daily 10–7; May and Sept., daily 10–6; Apr. and Oct., weekends 10–6.*

FOLLY BEACH COUNTY PARK, 12 mi south of Charleston via U.S. 17 and Route 171 (Folly Road), has 4,000 ft of ocean frontage and 2,000 ft of river frontage. Lifeguards are on duty seasonally. Facilities include dressing areas, outdoor showers, rest rooms, and picnicking areas; beach chair, raft, and umbrella rentals; and parking. *1100 W. Ashley Ave., Folly Island, tel. 843/588–2426. $5 per car (up to 8 passengers). May–Aug., daily 9–7; Apr. and Sept.–Oct., daily 10–6; Nov.–Mar., daily 10–5.*

ISLE OF PALMS COUNTY PARK is on the Isle of Palms at the foot of the Isle of Palms connector. Lifeguards are on duty seasonally along a 600-ft section of the beach. Facilities include dressing areas, outdoor showers, rest rooms, picnicking areas, beach chair and raft rentals, and a 350-vehicle parking lot. *1 14th Ave., Isle of Palms, Mount Pleasant/East Cooper, tel. 843/886–3863. $5 per car (up to 8 passengers). May–Aug., daily 9–7; Apr. and Sept.–Oct., daily 10–6; Nov.–Mar., daily 10–5.*

BIKING

The historic district is ideal for bicycling as long as you stay off the main, busy roads; many city parks have biking trails. Palmetto Islands County Park also has trails. Bikes can be rented at the **BICYCLE SHOPPE** (280 Meeting St., Market area, tel. 843/722–8168; also Kiawah Island, tel. 843/768–9122). **ISLAND BIKE AND SURF SHOP** (Kiawah Island, tel. 843/768–1158) rents bikes, surfboards, and Rollerblades. You'll get a better deal at **ALLIGATOR BIKE** (1823 Paulette Dr., Johns Island, tel. 843/559–8200), which serves Kiawah and Seabrook islands. **SEA ISLAND CYCLE** (4053 Rhett Ave., North Charleston, tel. 843/747–2453) serves all the local islands.

GOLF

One of the most appealing aspects of golfing in the Charleston area is the relaxing pace. With fewer golfers playing the courses than in destinations that are primarily golf oriented, players find choice starting times and an unhurried environment. Nonguests may play on a space-available basis at private island resorts, such as Kiawah Island, Seabrook Island, and Wild Dunes. Top public courses in the area are 18-hole, par-72 courses. For a listing of area golf packages, contact **CHARLESTON GOLF INC.** (tel. 800/774–4444).

The prestigious Pete Dye–designed **OCEAN COURSE AT KIAWAH ISLAND RESORT** (1000 Ocean Course Dr., Kiawah Island, tel. 843/768–7272) is an 18-hole, par-72 course that was the site of the 1991 Ryder Cup. Championship **KIAWAH COURSES,** all 18 holes and par 72, are the Gary Player–designed Marsh Point; Osprey Point, by Tom Fazio; and Turtle Point, a Jack Nicklaus layout (for all three: 12 Kiawah Beach Dr.). **SEABROOK ISLAND RESORT,** a secluded hideaway on Johns Island, offers two more 18-hole, par-72 championship courses: Crooked Oaks, by Robert Trent Jones Sr., and Ocean Winds, designed by William Byrd (for both: Seabrook Island Rd., tel. 843/768–2529). **WILD DUNES RESORT,** on the Isle of Palms, has two 18-hole, par-72 Tom Fazio designs: the Links (10001 Back Bay Dr., Mount Pleasant/East Cooper, tel. 843/886–2180) and Harbor Course (5881 Palmetto Dr., Mount Pleasant/East Cooper, tel. 843/886–2301).

CHARLESTON MUNICIPAL (2110 Maybank Hwy., James Island, tel. 843/795–6517) is a public, walker-friendly course. **CHARLESTON NATIONAL COUNTRY CLUB** (1360 National Dr., Mount Pleasant/East Cooper, tel. 843/884–7799) is well maintained and tends to be quiet on weekdays. The **DUNES WEST GOLF CLUB** (3535 Wando Plantation Way, Mount Pleasant/East Cooper, tel. 843/856–9000) has great marshland views and lots of modulation on the greens. **LINKS AT STONO FERRY** (5365 Forest Oaks Dr., Hollywood, tel. 843/763–1817) is a popular public course with great rates. **OAK POINT GOLF COURSE** (4255 Bohicket Rd., Johns Island, tel. 843/768–7431) has water on 16 holes, narrow fairways, and lots of chances to spot wildlife. **PATRIOTS POINT** (1 Patriots Point Rd., Mount Pleasant/East Cooper, tel. 843/881–0042) has a partly covered driving range and spectacular harbor views. **SHADOWMOSS GOLF CLUB** (20 Dunvegan Dr., West Ashley, tel. 843/556–8251) is a well-marked, forgiving course with one of the best finishing holes in the area.

HORSEBACK RIDING

M & M FARMS (Mount Pleasant/East Cooper, tel. 843/336–4886), in the National Forest Equestrian Center of Francis Marion Forest, offers guided trail tours. **SEABROOK ISLAND EQUESTRIAN CENTER** (Seabrook Island, tel. 843/768–7541) is open to the public and offers trail rides on the beach and through maritime forests and has pony rides for the kids.

SCUBA DIVING

The **COOPER RIVER UNDERWATER HERITAGE DIVING TRAIL** is more than 2 mi long and consists of six submerged sites, including ships that date to the Revolutionary War. Contact the **EAST COAST DIVE CONNECTION** (206B E. 5th North St., Hwy. 78, Summerville, tel. 843/821–0001) for lessons, rentals, and information. **CHARLESTON SCUBA** (335 Savannah Hwy., West Ashley, tel. 843/763–3483) for maps, rentals, and excursion information.

TENNIS

You can play for free at neighborhood courts, including several across the street from Colonial Lake and at the Isle of Palms

Recreation Center on the Isle of Palms. Courts are open to the public at **KIAWAH ISLAND** (tel. 843/768–2121). **SHADOWMOSS PLANTATION** (tel. 843/556–8251) has public courts available. **WILD DUNES** (tel. 843/886–6000) is a swanky resort with nice courts and a full tennis shop. **MAYBANK TENNIS CENTER** (1880 Houghton Dr., James Island, tel. 843/406–8814) has lights on its six courts. **CHARLESTON TENNIS CENTER** (19 Farmfield Ave., West Ashley, tel. 843/724–7402) is a city facility with lots of courts and locker rooms. The Family Circle Cup takes place at the **TOWN CENTER PARK ON DANIEL ISLAND** (tel. 843/534–2400), a 32-acre tennis and recreational park with a racquet club and 17 public tennis courts.

NIGHTLIFE AND THE ARTS

THE ARTS

Concerts

The **CHARLESTON CONCERT ASSOCIATION** (tel. 843/722–7667) has information on visiting performing arts groups including symphonies, ballets, and operas. The **CHARLESTON SYMPHONY ORCHESTRA** (843/723–7528) presents MasterWorks Series, Downtown Pops, Family Series, and an annual holiday concert at Gaillard Municipal Auditorium (77 Calhoun St., Upper King, tel. 843/577–4500). The orchestra also performs the Sotille Chamber Series at the Sotille Theater (44 George St., Market area, tel. 843/953–6340) and the Light and Lively Pops at Charleston Southern University (U.S. 78, tel. 843/953–6340). The College of Charleston has a free **MONDAY NIGHT RECITAL SERIES** (tel. 843/953–8228).

Dance

ANONYMITY DANCE COMPANY (tel. 843/886–6104), a modern dance troupe, performs throughout the city. The **CHARLESTON BALLET THEATRE** (477 King St., Upper King, tel. 843/723–7334) performs everything from classical to contemporary dance at locations around the city. The **ROBERT IVEY BALLET COMPANY** (tel. 843/556–1343), a semiprofessional company that includes College of Charleston students, gives a fall and spring program of jazz, classical, and modern dance at the Sotille Theater (44 George St., Market area, tel. 843/953–6340).

Festivals

The **FALL CANDLELIGHT TOURS OF HOMES AND GARDENS** (tel. 843/722–4630), sponsored by the Preservation Society of Charleston in September and October, offers an inside look at Charleston's private buildings and gardens.

During the **FESTIVAL OF HOUSES AND GARDENS** (tel. 843/724–8484), held during March and April each year, more than 100 private homes, gardens, and historic churches are open to the public for tours sponsored by the Historic Charleston Foundation. There are also symphony galas in stately drawing rooms, plantation oyster roasts, and candlelight tours.

The **MOJA ARTS FESTIVAL** (tel. 843/724–7305), which takes place during the last week of September and first week of October, celebrates the rich heritage of the African continent and Caribbean influences on African-American culture. It includes theater, dance, and music performances; art shows; films; lectures; and tours of the historic district.

PICCOLO SPOLETO FESTIVAL (tel. 843/724–7305) is the spirited companion festival of Spoleto Festival USA, showcasing the best in local and regional talent from every artistic discipline. There are about 300 events—from jazz performances to puppet shows—held at 60 sites in 17 days from mid-May through early June, and most performances are free.

The **SOUTHEASTERN WILDLIFE EXPOSITION** (tel. 843/723–1748 or 800/221–5273), in mid-February, is one of Charleston's biggest annual events. You'll find art by renowned wildlife artists, live animal demonstrations, and a chili cook-off.

SPOLETO FESTIVAL USA (tel. 843/722–2764), founded by the composer Gian Carlo Menotti in 1977, has become a world-famous celebration of the arts. For two weeks, from late May to early June, opera, dance, theater, symphonic and chamber music, jazz, and the visual arts are showcased in concert halls, theaters, parks, churches, streets, and gardens throughout the city.

Film

The **AMERICAN THEATER** (446 King St., Upper King, tel. 843/722–3456), a renovated theater from the 1940s, shows current movies in a table-and-chairs setting with pizza, burgers, finger foods, beer, and wine. Upstairs there's a virtual reality game center. IMAX fans should check out the **IMAX THEATER** (360 Concord St., Upper King, tel. 843/725–4629) next to the South Carolina Aquarium.

Theater

Several groups, including the Footlight Players and Charleston Stage Company, perform at the **DOCK STREET THEATRE** (135 Church St., Market area, tel. 843/723–5648). **PLUFF MUD PRODUCTIONS** puts on comedies at the Isle of Palms Windjammer (1000 Ocean Blvd., Mount Pleasant/East Cooper, tel. 843/886–8596). The Footlight Players regularly perform at the **FOOTLIGHT PLAYERS THEATRE** (20 Queen St., Market area, tel. 843/722–4487). Performances by the College of Charleston's theater department and guest theatrical groups are presented during the school year at the **SIMONS CENTER FOR THE ARTS** (54 St. Phillips St., Market area, tel. 843/953–5604).

NIGHTLIFE

Dancing and Music

CUMBERLAND'S (26 Cumberland St., Market area, tel. 843/577–9469) has live blues, rock, reggae, and bluegrass; the place is also known for buffalo wings and cheap beer. There's live music and dancing at the **CITY BAR** (5 Faber St., Market area, tel. 843/577–7383) each weekend. The **MILLS HOUSE HOTEL** (115 Meeting St., Market area, tel. 843/577–2400), favored by an elegant, mature crowd, has a lively bar. Most evenings **MOMMA'S BLUES PALACE** (46 John St., Upper King, tel. 843/853–2221) has live music starting at 10 PM. The cavernous **MUSIC FARM** (32 Ann St., Upper King, tel. 843/853–3276), in a renovated train station, showcases live national and local alternative bands. There are dancing and funky '70s music at **TRIO CLUB** (139 Calhoun St., Upper King, tel. 843/965–5333) Wednesday through Saturday. The **WINDJAMMER** (1000 Ocean Blvd., Mount Pleasant/East Cooper, tel. 843/886–8596), on the Isle of Palms, is an oceanfront spot with live rock. Nearby on Sullivan's Island, **BERT'S BAR** (2209 Middle St., Mount Pleasant/East Cooper, tel. 843/883–3924), a true beach-bum neighborhood joint, has live music on weekends and a great all-you-can-eat fish fry on Friday night from 6 to 9.

Dinner Cruises

For an evening of dining and dancing, climb aboard the luxury yacht **SPIRIT OF CAROLINA** (tel. 843/722–2628). Reservations are essential; there are no cruises Sunday and Monday. Breakfast, brunch, deli, and hot luncheons are prepared on board the **CHARLESTOWNE PRINCESS** (tel. 843/722–1112), which also offers its Harborlites Dinner with live entertainment and dancing while cruising the harbor and rivers.

Hotel and Jazz Bars

The **BEST FRIEND LOUNGE** (115 Meeting St., Market area, tel. 843/577–2400), in the Mills House Hotel, has a guitarist playing light tunes most nights. The elegant **CHARLESTON GRILL** (224 King St., Market area, tel. 843/577–4522), in Charleston Place, offers live jazz nightly. In the **LOBBY LOUNGE** (130 Market St., Market area, tel. 843/722–4900), on Charleston Place, afternoon high tea, cocktails, and appetizers are accompanied by piano. At **MISTRAL RESTAURANT** (99 S. Market St., Market area, tel. 843/722–5709) there's a regular four-piece jazz band on weekends. **MITCHELL'S** (102 N. Market St., Market area, tel. 843/722–0732) has nightly acts, from jazz pianists to Latin dance bands.

Lounges and Bars/Breweries

CHARLIE'S LITTLE BAR (141 E. Bay St., Market area, tel. 843/723–6242), above Saracen Restaurant, is intimate, cozy, and popular with young professionals. **CLUB HABANA** (177 Meeting St., Market area, tel. 843/853–5900) is a chic wood-paneled martini bar (open late) with a cigar shop downstairs. **SOUTHEND BREWERY** (161 E. Bay St., Market area, tel. 843/853–4677) has a lively bar with beer brewed on the premises; the food is good, especially the soups. You'll find authentic Irish music at **TOMMY CONDON'S IRISH PUB & RESTAURANT** (160 Church St., Market area, tel. 843/577–3818). **VICKERY'S BAR & GRILL** (139 Calhoun St., Market area, tel. 843/723–1558) is a festive nightspot with a spacious outdoor patio and good late-night food. There's another equally popular location in Mount

Pleasant (1205 Shrimp Boat La., Mount Pleasant/East Cooper, tel. 843/849–6770).

WHERE TO STAY

Rates tend to be highest during the spring and fall (except at resort areas, when summer is high season) and during special events, including the Spring Festival of Houses and Spoleto—when reservations are essential.

CATEGORY	COST*
$$$$	over $200
$$$	$150–$200
$$	$100–$150
$	under $100

*All prices are for a standard double room, excluding 7% tax.

HOTELS AND MOTELS

$$$$ **BEST WESTERN KING CHARLES INN.** This inn in the historic district is a cut above the typical chain, with a welcoming lobby and sitting area and spacious rooms furnished with 18th-century period reproductions. *237 Meeting St., Market area, 29401, tel. 843/723–7451 or 800/528–1234, fax 843/723–2041, www. kingcharlesinn.com. 91 rooms. Restaurant, in-room data ports, pool, free parking. AE, D, DC, MC, V.*

$$$$ **CHARLESTON PLACE.** This Orient-Express property, a graceful low-
★   rise structure in the historic district, is surrounded by upscale boutiques and specialty shops. The lobby has a magnificent handblown Venetian-glass chandelier, an Italian marble floor, and antiques from Sotheby's. Rooms are furnished with period reproductions, linen sheets and robes, and fax machines. Overall, this hotel is simply world class. *130 Market St., Market area, 29401, tel. 843/722–4900 or 800/611–5545, fax 843/724–7215, www. charlestonplacehotel.com. 400 rooms, 40 suites. 2 restaurants, minibars,*

2 tennis courts, indoor pool, hot tub, health club, spa, bar, lobby lounge, concierge, concierge floor, business services, meeting rooms. AE, D, DC, MC, V.

$$$–$$$$ EMBASSY SUITES HISTORIC CHARLESTON. The courtyard of the Old Citadel military school where cadets once marched is now a skylighted atrium with stone floors, armchairs, palm trees, and a fountain. The restored brick walls of the breakfast room and some guest rooms in this contemporary hotel contain original gun ports, reminders that the 1822 building was originally a fortification. Teak and mahogany furniture, safari motifs, and sisal carpeting recall the British colonial era. Breakfast and evening refreshments are complimentary. 341 Meeting St., Upper King, 29403, tel. 843/723–6900 or 800/362–2779, fax 843/723–6938, www.embassysuites.com. 153 suites. Restaurant, room service, some in-room hot tubs, outdoor hot tubs, microwaves, refrigerators, pool, gym, lounge, shop, meeting rooms, business services. AE, D, DC, MC, V. BP.

$$$–$$$$ HAMPTON INN–HISTORIC DISTRICT. This downtown chain has
★ hardwood floors and a fireplace in the elegant lobby, guest rooms with period reproductions, and a courtyard garden. It's also conveniently near a DASH shuttle stop. 345 Meeting St., Upper King, 29403, tel. 843/723–4000 or 800/426–7866, fax 843/722–3725, www.hamptoninn.com. 166 rooms, 5 suites. Some refrigerators, some microwaves, pool, meeting rooms. AE, D, DC, MC, V. CP.

$$$–$$$$ HARBORVIEW INN. Overlooking the harbor and Waterfront Park, this inn is close to most downtown attractions. Calming earth tones and rattan are abundant; high ceilings, four-poster beds, and seagrass rugs complete the Lowcountry look. Some of the rooms are in a former 19th-century shipping warehouse with exposed brick walls; some have fireplaces and whirlpool tubs. Afternoon wine and cheese as well as evening cookies are included. 2 Vendue Range, Market area, 29401, tel. 843/853–8439 or 888/853–8439, fax 843/853–4034, www.charlestonmanagement.com/hvi. 51 rooms, 1 suite. Some in-room hot tubs, in-room data ports, concierge, business services. AE, D, DC, MC, V. CP.

$$$–$$$$ MILLS HOUSE HOTEL. Antique furnishings and period decor give this luxurious Holiday Inn property plenty of charm. It's a reconstruction of an old hostelry on its original site in the historic district, and although rooms are small and a bit standard, the hotel has a lounge with live entertainment and a nice dining room. *115 Meeting St., Market area, 29401, tel. 843/577–2400 or 800/874–9600, fax 843/722–0623, www.millshouse.com. 199 rooms, 16 suites. Pool, restaurant, room service, bar, lounge, concierge, concierge floor, business services, meeting rooms, parking (fee). AE, D, DC, MC, V.*

$$–$$$$ DOUBLETREE GUEST SUITES HISTORIC CHARLESTON. Across from the City Market, this hotel has a restored entrance portico from an 1874 bank, a refurbished 1866 firehouse, and three lush gardens. The spacious suites, all decorated with 18th-century reproductions and canopy beds, have wet bars with microwave ovens and refrigerators. *181 Church St., Market area, 29401, tel. 843/577–2644 or 877/408–8733, fax 843/577–2697, www.doubletree.com. 182 suites. Gym, lounge, business services, meeting room. AE, D, DC, MC, V.*

$$$ MEETING STREET INN. Built in 1874, this salmon-color former tavern in the historic district overlooks a lovely courtyard with fountains and gardens. Spacious rooms have hardwood floors, high ceilings, and reproduction furniture including four-poster rice beds. *173 Meeting St., Market area, 29401, tel. 843/723–1882 or 800/842–8022, fax 843/577–0851, www.meetingstreetinn.com. 54 rooms. Some refrigerators, outdoor hot tub, bar. AE, D, DC, MC, V. CP.*

$$–$$$ HOLIDAY INN CHARLESTON/MOUNT PLEASANT. Just over the Cooper River Bridge, the Holiday Inn is a 10-minute drive from the downtown historic district. Everything has been gracefully done: big banana trees in the lobby, brass lamps, crystal chandeliers, contemporary furniture. *250 U.S. 17, Mount Pleasant/East Cooper 29464, tel. 843/884–6000 or 800/290–4004, fax 843/881–1786, www.holidayinn-mtpleasant.com. 158 rooms. Restaurant, some*

refrigerators and microwaves, pool, gym, sauna, lounge, meeting room.
AE, D, DC, MC, V.

$$–$$$ **WESTIN FRANCIS MARION HOTEL.** Built in 1924 as the largest
★ hotel in the Carolinas, the restored Francis Marion is now a Westin
property. However, it has retained its big-band and tea-dance
glamour with its windowed ballrooms, wrought-iron railings,
columns, high ceilings, crown moldings, decorative plasterwork,
and views of Marion Square and the harbor. Excellent Southern
cuisine can be had at Elliott's on the Square. *387 King St., Upper
King, 29403, tel. 843/722–0600 or 888/625–5144, fax 843/723–
4633, www.westinfm.com. 160 rooms, 66 suites. Restaurant, coffee shop,
in-room data ports, gym, lounge, Internet, concierge, business services,
meeting rooms, parking (fee).* AE, D, DC, MC, V.

$$ **HOLIDAY INN HISTORIC DISTRICT.** Although this hotel changed
hands and went through a major renovation, it still draws loyal
repeat visitors because of its free parking and location—a block
from the Gaillard Municipal Auditorium and within walking
distance of many must-see spots. Rooms are motel modern. *125
Calhoun St., Upper King, 29401, tel. 843/805–7900 or 877/805–7900,
fax 843/805–7700, www.charlestonhotel.com. 126 rooms. Restaurant,
in-room data ports, pool, bar, concierge, concierge floor, Internet, business
services, meeting rooms, parking.* AE, D, DC, MC, V.

$–$$ **HAMPTON INN CHARLESTON–NORTH.** This upscale Hampton
Inn, just off Ashley Phosphate Rd., has a grand marble lobby, a
solarium overlooking the pool, crown moldings, and Lowcountry-
style furniture. The mostly business clientele rates it tops for
service and design. *7424 Northside Dr., North Charleston, 29420,
tel. 843/820–2030 or 877/870–2030, fax 843/820–2010,
www.hamptoninncharleston.com. 102 rooms. In-room data ports, some
hot tubs, some kitchens, in-room VCRs, pool, gym, business services,
laundry service, meeting room.* AE, D, DC, MC, V.

$ RED ROOF INN. At the foot of the Cooper River Bridge in Mt. Pleasant, about 10 minutes from historic Charleston, this chain motel is clean and well lighted. Some rooms have work areas. *301 Johnnie Dodds Blvd., Mount Pleasant/East Cooper, 29403, tel. 843/ 884–1411 or 800/843–7663, fax 843/884–1411, www.redroof.com. 124 rooms. Pool, some refrigerators, some microwaves. AE, D, DC, MC, V.*

INNS AND GUEST HOUSES

$$$$ JOHN RUTLEDGE HOUSE INN. This 1763 house, built by John
★ Rutledge, one of the framers of the U.S. Constitution, is one of Charleston's most luxurious inns. The ornate ironwork, original woodwork, plaster moldings, parquet floors, marble fireplaces, and 14-ft ceilings are impressive. A lovely afternoon tea including wine is served in the ballroom, and a Continental breakfast is served—on the patio, if you prefer sitting outside. Newspapers are delivered to your room. Some guest rooms have fireplaces. There are also two charming period carriage houses that you can stay in. *116 Broad St., South of Broad, 29401, tel. 843/723–7999 or 800/476–9741, fax 843/720–2615, www.charminginns.com. 11 rooms in mansion, 4 in each of 2 carriage houses. Some hot tubs, refrigerators, business services. AE, D, DC, MC, V. CP.*

$$$$ PLANTERS INN. High-ceiling rooms and suites are beautifully appointed with opulent furnishings, including mahogany four-poster beds and marble baths. Twenty-one rooms have a piazza overlooking the garden courtyard. The inn's Peninsula Grill is wonderful. *112 N. Market St., Market area, 29401, tel. 843/722–2345 or 800/845–7082, fax 843/577–2125, www.plantersinn.com. 56 rooms, 6 suites. Restaurant, some hot tubs, room service, concierge, business services; no-smoking floors. AE, D, DC, MC, V.*

$$$$ WENTWORTH MANSION. This spectacular brick mansion, built around 1886 as a private home, is now a luxury inn. Hand-carved marble fireplaces, rich woodwork, chandeliers, 14-ft ceilings, and Second Empire reproductions create a sense of elegance in the spacious guest rooms. Breakfast buffet, evening wine and cheese, sherry, and turndown service are included. Rooms have king-size beds and CD players; most have gas fireplaces and some have daybeds. Circa 1886, in the former carriage house, serves inventive food and is the perfect spot for a special occasion. *149 Wentworth St., College of Charleston, 29403, tel. 843/853-1886 or 888/466-1886, fax 843/723-8634, www.wentworthmansion.com. 21 rooms. Restaurant, hot tubs, lounge, free parking. AE, D, DC, MC, V. BP.*

$$$–$$$$ **ANSONBOROUGH INN.** Formerly a stationer's warehouse dating from the early 1900s, this spacious all-suites inn is furnished in period reproductions. It offers hair dryers, irons, a morning newspaper, message service, wine reception, and rooftop terrace, but it's best known for its friendly staff. *21 Hasell St., Market area, 29401, tel. 843/723-1655 or 800/522-2073, fax 843/527-6888, www.ansonboroughinn.com. 37 suites. Bar, meeting room. AE, MC, V. CP.*

$$$–$$$$ **HAYNE HOUSE.** One block from the Battery, in Charleston's prestigious South of Broad neighborhood, the Hayne House was built in 1755. It has old furnishings but a fresh, light spirit. Rooms have federal antiques and other heirlooms from the proprietors' families. Two of the guest rooms are in the main house; the other four are in the kitchen house, with its narrow stairway, colonial brickwork, and chimney. *30 King St., South of Broad, 29401, tel. 843/577-2633, fax 843/577-5906, www.haynehouse.com. 4 rooms, 2 suites. MC, V. CP.*

$$$–$$$$ **PHOEBE PEMBER HOUSE.** Built in 1807, the mansion has a separate carriage house, which has two guest rooms upstairs and a living room, dining room, kitchenette, and garden downstairs. Colors and fabrics are cheerful yet refined; artwork is by Charleston artists. The inn is off a busy street, but the piazza is cocooned by a walled garden overlooking Charleston's port. A nearby studio offers yoga classes and workshops. *26 Society St., Market area, 29401, tel. 843/722–4186, fax 843/722–0557, www. phoebepemberhouse.com. 6 rooms. Massage, free parking; no smoking. AE, MC, V. CP.*

$$$–$$$$ **TWO MEETING STREET.** As pretty as a wedding cake and just as
★ romantic, this early 20th-century inn on the Battery has two suites with working fireplaces and balconies. In the public spaces there are Tiffany windows, carved English oak paneling, and a chandelier from the former Czechoslovakia. Expect to be treated to afternoon high tea and a Continental breakfast. *2 Meeting St., South of Broad, 29401, tel. 843/723–7322, www.twomeetingstreet.com. 7 rooms, 2 suites. No credit cards. CP.*

$$$ **CANNONBORO INN AND ASHLEY INN.** Two of the most elegant inns in town, these B&B neighbors on the edge of the historic district near the Medical University of South Carolina have luxurious rooms, tastefully decorated in period furnishings. Expect to be treated to a full English breakfast on a piazza overlooking the Charleston gardens. Use of the bicycles and afternoon refreshments are included. *Cannonboro: 184 Ashley Ave., Medical University of South Carolina, 29403, tel. 843/723–8572, fax 843/723–8007, www.charleston-sc-inns.com. 6 rooms. Bicycles, business services, free parking. MC, V. BP. Ashley: 201 Ashley Ave., Medical University of South Carolina, 29403, tel. 843/723–1848, fax 843/579–9080. 6 rooms, 1 suite. Bicycles, business services, free parking. AE, D, MC, V. BP.*

$$$ **VENDUE INN.** This elegant yet friendly inn is close to the harbor and Waterfront Park (though its views are now obstructed by a condo building). Guest rooms have four-poster beds, cozy seating areas, and large bathrooms. A full buffet breakfast, afternoon wine and cheese, and evening milk and cookies are complimentary. The inn's rooftop terrace bar has sweeping harbor views. *19 Vendue Range, Market area, 29401, tel. 843/577–7970 or 800/845–7900, www.vendueinn.com. 31 rooms, 35 suites. Restaurant, in-room data ports, bicycles, bar, business services, meeting room. AE, D, DC, MC, V. BP.*

\$\$–\$\$\$ **1837 BED AND BREAKFAST AND TEA ROOM.** Although not as fancy as some of the B&Bs in town, this inn has an extremely hospitable staff; you'll get a sense of what it's really like to live in one of Charleston's beloved homes. Restored and operated by two artists-teachers, the home and carriage house have rooms filled with antiques, including romantic canopied beds. The delicious breakfast includes homemade breads and hot entrées such as sausage pie or ham frittatas. *126 Wentworth St., Market area, 29401, tel. 843/723–7166 or 877/723–1837, fax 843/722–7179, www. 1837bb.com. 8 rooms, 1 suite. AE, D, MC, V. BP.*

\$\$–\$\$\$ **ELLIOTT HOUSE INN.** Listen to the chimes of St. Michael's Episcopal Church as you sip wine in the courtyard of this lovely old inn in the heart of the historic district. You can then retreat to a cozy room with period furniture, including canopied four-posters and Oriental carpets. *78 Queen St., Market area, 29401, tel. 843/723–1855 or 800/729–1855, fax 843/722–1567, www. elliotthouseinn.com. 24 rooms. Hot tub, bicycles. AE, D, MC, V. CP.*

\$\$–\$\$\$ **GUILDS INN.** An easygoing elegance characterizes this place in Mount Pleasant's historic and scenic Old Village, a residential area with a pharmacy whose soda fountain will take you back in time. The National Historic Register property has hardwood floors, traditional Lowcountry furnishings, and a mix of antiques and reproductions. Rooms have whirlpool tubs. Although the self-serve morning pastries are grocery store–bought, the laid-back management is part of the unstuffy charm of this inn. *101 Pitt St., Mount Pleasant/East Cooper, 29464, tel. 843/881–0510 or 800/569–4038, fax 843/884–5020, www.guildsinn.com. 5 rooms, 1 suite. AE, D, MC, V. CP.*

RESORT ISLANDS

On the semitropical islands dotting the South Carolina coast near Charleston you'll find several sumptuous resorts that offer lots of different packages. Peak season rates (during spring and summer vacations) range from $140 to $300 per day, double occupancy for stays up to five nights; rates drop for weekly stays and during off-season.

$$$$ WILD DUNES. This 1,600-acre resort on the Isle of Palms has one- to six-bedroom villas and homes for rent, plus the plantation-style Boardwalk Inn. Rental locations range from oceanfront to courtside to marsh-side. The inn is just off the beach, in a relaxing boardwalk cluster of villas and shops; guest rooms have balconies and overlook the ocean. Nearby is a yacht harbor on the Intracoastal Waterway. You have a long list of recreational options here. *Palm Blvd. at 41st Ave., Isle of Palms (Box 20575, Charleston 29413), tel. 843/886–6000 or 888/845–8926, fax 843/886–2916, www.wilddunes.com. 430 units, 93 rooms. 2 restaurants, pizzeria, snack bar, ice cream parlor, fans, some in-room hot tubs, 2 18-hole golf courses, 17 tennis courts, 4 pools, indoor pool, wading pool, health club, boating, fishing, bicycles, volleyball, lounge, video game room, children's programs (ages 3–12), concierge, meeting rooms, airport shuttle. AE, D, DC, MC, V.*

$$$–$$$$ KIAWAH ISLAND RESORT. Choose from newly renovated inn rooms and completely equipped one- to five-bedroom villas and private homes in two luxurious resort villages on 10,000 wooded acres. There are 10 mi of fine broad beaches and plenty of recreational opportunities. Dining options are many and varied. *12 Kiawah Beach Dr., Kiawah Island 29455, tel. 843/768–2121 or 800/654–2924, fax 843/768–6099, www.kiawahresort.com. 150 rooms, 430 villas and private homes. 8 restaurants, 5 18-hole golf courses, 28 tennis courts, pro shop, 5 pools, wading pool, boating, fishing, bicycles, lounges, shops, children's programs (ages 3–12). AE, D, DC, MC, V.*

$$$–$$$$ SEABROOK ISLAND RESORT. About 200 completely equipped one- to six-bedroom villas, cottages, and beach houses occupy this property (the number varies according to how many homeowners sign up for the rental program). The resort is noted for its secluded wooded areas and abundance of wildlife—look for bobcats and white-tailed deer. The Beach Club and Island House, open to guests, are centers for dining and leisure activities. Bohicket Marina Village, the hub of activity around the island, offers restaurants as well as pizza and sub shops, plus opportunities for scuba diving, deep-sea- and inshore-fishing charters, and small-boat rentals. *1002 Landfall Way, Seabrook Island 29455, tel. 843/768–1000 or 800/845–2475, fax 843/768–3096, www.seabrookresort.com. 200 units. 3 restaurants, 2 18-hole golf courses, 13 tennis courts, 2 pools, wading pool, boating, parasailing, fishing, bicycles, horseback riding, children's programs. AE, D, DC, MC, V.*

practical information

Air Travel

BOOKING

Price is just one factor to consider when booking a flight: frequency of service and even a carrier's safety record are often just as important. Major airlines offer the greatest number of departures. Smaller airlines—including regional and no-frills airlines—usually have a limited number of flights daily. On the other hand, low-cost airlines usually are cheaper, and their fares impose fewer restrictions, such as advance-purchase requirements. Safetywise, low-cost carriers as a group have a good history—about equal to that of major carriers.

When you book **look for nonstop flights** and **remember that "direct" flights stop at least once.** Try to avoid connecting flights, which require a change of plane. For more booking tips and to check prices and make on-line flight reservations, log on to www.fodors.com.

CARRIERS

Savannah is served by AirTran Airways, ASA, Comair, Continental Express, Delta, United Express, and US Airways/Express for domestic flights. Glynco Jetport in the coastal isles is served by Delta affiliate Atlantic Southeast Airlines (ASA), with flights from Atlanta.

Charleston is served by AirTran Airways, ASA, Comair, Continental Express, Delta, United Express, and US Airways/Express for domestic flights.

➤**MAJOR AIRLINES: Air Canada** (tel. 800/776–3000). **American** (tel. 800/433–7300). **British Airways** (tel. 0345/222–111). **Continental** (tel. 800/525–0280). **Delta** (tel. 800/221–1212). **Northwest Airlines/KLM** (tel. 800/225–2525). **United** (tel. 800/241–6522). **US Airways** (tel. 800/428–4322).

➤**SMALLER AIRLINES: AirTran** (tel. 770/994–8258 or 800/247–8726). **Atlantic Southeast/Delta Connection** (tel. 800/221–1212 or 800/282–3424). **ComAir** (tel. 800/221–1212). **Continental Express** (tel. 800/525–0280). **Midway** (tel. 800/446–4392). **Midwest Express** (tel. 800/452–2022).

CHECK-IN AND BOARDING

Assuming that not everyone with a ticket will show up, airlines routinely overbook planes. When everyone does, airlines ask for volunteers to give up their seats. In return, these volunteers usually get a certificate for a free flight and are rebooked on the next flight out. If there are not enough volunteers, the airline must choose who will be denied boarding. The first to get bumped are passengers who checked in late and those flying on discounted tickets, so **get to the gate and check in as early as possible,** especially during peak periods.

Always **bring a government-issued photo I.D. to the airport;** even when it's not required, a passport is best.

CUTTING COSTS

The least expensive airfares to the Carolinas and Georgia usually must be purchased in advance and are nonrefundable. It's smart to **call a number of airlines,** and when you are quoted a good price, **book it on the spot**—the same fare may not be available the next day. Always **check different routings** and look into using different airports. Travel agents, especially low-fare specialists (☞ Discounts & Deals), are helpful.

Consolidators are another good source. They buy tickets for scheduled international flights at reduced rates from the airlines, then sell them at prices that beat the best fare available directly from the airlines, usually without restrictions. Sometimes you can even get your money back if you need to return the ticket. Carefully read the fine print detailing penalties for changes and cancellations, and **confirm your consolidator reservation with the airline.**

➤**CONSOLIDATORS: Cheap Tickets** (tel. 800/377–1000). **Discount Airline Ticket Service** (tel. 800/576–1600). **Unitravel** (tel. 800/325–2222). **Up & Away Travel** (tel. 212/889–2345, www.upandaway.com). **World Travel Network** (tel. 800/409–6753).

ENJOYING THE FLIGHT

For more legroom, **request an emergency-aisle seat.** Don't sit in the row in front of the emergency aisle or in front of a bulkhead, where seats may not recline. If you have dietary concerns, **ask for special meals when booking.** These can be vegetarian, low-cholesterol, or kosher, for example. On long flights, try to maintain a normal routine, to help fight jet lag. At night, **get some sleep.** By day, **eat light meals, drink water** (not alcohol), and **move around the cabin** to stretch your legs. For additional jet-lag tips consult *Fodor's FYI: Travel Fit & Healthy* (available at bookstores everywhere).

HOW TO COMPLAIN

If your baggage goes astray or your flight goes awry, complain right away. Most carriers require that you **file a claim immediately.**

➤**AIRLINE COMPLAINTS: U.S. Department of Transportation Aviation Consumer Protection Division** (C-75, Room 4107, Washington, DC 20590, tel. 202/366–2220, www.dot.gov/airconsumer). **Federal Aviation Administration Consumer Hotline** (tel. 800/322–7873).

PRACTICAL INFORMATION • **123**

Airports and Transfers

Savannah International Airport is 18 mi west of downtown. Despite the name, international flights are nonexistent. The foreign trade zone, a locus for importing, constitutes the "international" aspect. The coastal isles are served by Glynco Jetport, 6 mi north of Brunswick near the coastal isles. Charleston International Airport on I–26, 12 mi west of downtown, is served by Continental, Comair, Delta, Midway Express, United Express, Northwest, TWA, and US Airways.

►**AIRPORT INFORMATION: Charleston International Airport** (5500 International Blvd., North Charleston, tel. 843/ 767–1100). **Glynco Jetport** (500 Connole St., tel. 912/ 265–2070, 800/235–0859, www.glynncountyairports.com). **Savannah International Airport** (400 Airways Ave., tel. 912/ 964–0514, www.savannahairport.com).

AIRPORT TRANSFERS

In Savannah, vans operated by McCall's Limousine Service leave the airport daily for downtown locations. The trip takes 15 minutes, and the one-way fare is $16 for one-way, $30 round-trip for one person; the two-person rate is $11 per person one-way, $22 per person round-trip. Routes can include other destinations in addition to downtown. Advance reservation is required.

Taxi service is an easy way to get from the airport to downtown Savannah; try AAA Adam Cab Incorporated and Yellow Cab Company; the one-way fare is about $20, plus $5 for each addition person. By car take I–95 south to I–16 east into downtown Savannah.

Several shuttle and cab companies service Charleston International Airport. It costs about $18–$22 to travel downtown by taxi; to Mount Pleasant, $23–$35. Fares are approximately $1.65 per mile. Airport Ground Transportation arranges shuttles, which cost $10 per person to the downtown area. Some hotels provide shuttle service.

➤TAXIS AND SHUTTLES: AAA Adam Cab Incorporated (tel. 912/927–7466). McCall's Limousine Service (tel. 912/966–5364). Yellow Cab Company (tel. 912/236–1133).

➤TAXIS AND SHUTTLES: Thurman's Limo (tel. 843/607–2912). Absolute Charleston (tel. 843/817–4044). Harvie's Taxi Limo Service (tel. 843/709–4276). Lee's Limousine (tel. 843/797–0041). Airport Ground Transportation (tel. 843/767–1100).

Bike Travel

Throughout coastal Georgia, South Carolina, and North Carolina, hills are few and the scenery remarkable. You'll find a number of extensive, in many cases marked, bike routes throughout North Carolina's Outer Banks, around Savannah and Georgia's coastal islands, and throughout greater Charleston and coastal South Carolina's Lowcountry. Serious enthusiasts, especially those of mountain biking, might take to the more precipitous parts of North Carolina and Georgia, which are the Great Smoky Mountains and north Georgia mountains, respectively.

There are dozens of local bike clubs throughout the area. To reach one of these groups, which generally welcome people who are visiting the area, and which can provide detailed advice on local routes and rental shops, contact the local tourist board or visit the appropriate tourism Web site (☞ Web sites), many of which have information on or links to area cycling resources. Many tourist boards also distribute bike maps.

BIKES IN FLIGHT

Most airlines accommodate bikes as luggage, provided they are dismantled and boxed. Airlines sell bike boxes, which are often free at bike shops, for about $5 (it's at least $100 for bike bags). International travelers can sometimes substitute a bike for a piece of checked luggage at no charge; otherwise, the cost is about $150. Domestic and Canadian airlines charge $50–$75.

Boat and Ferry Travel

Boaters on the Intracoastal Waterway may dock at Ashley Marina and City Marina, in Charleston Harbor, or at Wild Dunes Yacht Harbor, on the Isle of Palms.

CHARTS is the only full-service water taxi providing transportation to and from Patriots Point naval and maritime museum. It also offers harbor cruises.

Books, Movies, and Music

The South has a substantial literary heritage: novels, drama, and poetry, as well as short stories and songs. Its authors have many a Pulitzer to their names, among them Georgia-born Caroline Miller for fiction (*Lamb in His Bosom*, 1934). You can choose from works by Thomas Wolfe, Reynolds Price, Pat Conroy, and Flannery O'Connor, to name just a few. Charles Frazier's 1997 novel *Cold Mountain*, about the journeys of a Confederate soldier in western North Carolina, won a National Book Award.

The area has produced writers of popular fiction as varied as Margaret Mitchell (*Gone With the Wind*), Kaye Gibbons, and Anne Rivers Siddons. Although not authored by a Southerner, John Berendt's nonfiction *Midnight in the Garden of Good and Evil* is a tale of modern-day mayhem in sultry Savannah that reads like a novel.

One important element in Southern culture is the region's passion for history, defined as both personal, family history and regional history, which to those who live these means both personal family and the history of the region. To understand the importance of the Civil War period, view Ken Burns's nine-episode PBS television documentary *The Civil War*. Shelby Foote's three-volume history, *The Civil War*, is excellent, as is James McPherson's one-volume *Battle Cry of Freedom*, another history of the war.

The classic treatise on the culture of the South is W. J. Cash's groundbreaking *The Mind of the South*, published more than 50 years ago. The *Oxford Book of the American South*, edited by Edward L. Ayers and Bradley C. Mittendorf, is an outstanding collection of Southern writing about the region from the 18th century to the present.

Alfred Uhry's *Driving Miss Daisy*, a Pulitzer Prize—winning play and award-winning film, portrays an aspect of relationships between the races in the South. Black Southern writers, of both fiction and nonfiction, are now, increasingly, getting the recognition they deserve. Although she currently lives in San Francisco, Alice Walker (from Eatonton, Georgia) made her mark with the book *The Color Purple*, later a film. Maya Angelou is one of the region's most celebrated poets.

For more recent examples of the region's rich literary tradition, look no farther than *New Stories from the South*, an annual compendium of the best fiction from Southern writers, edited by Shannon Ravenel. In the anthology *Rebel Yell: Stories by Contemporary Southern Gay Authors*, editor Jay Quinn chooses authors who explore themes of growing up, falling in love, and accepting themselves in a part of the world that has not always been especially tolerant of gays and lesbians.

Some of the misconceptions about the South persisted as a result of the James Dickey novel-turned-movie *Deliverance*, about a group of friends on a canoeing trip in Georgia backcountry. Also originally a novel, the film *To Kill a Mockingbird* not only crystallizes the depths of prejudice and bigotry in the South, but also conveys a message of hope as a region struggles to come to terms with its past.

When it comes to music, you'll find that some of the biggest names across multiple genres were born and bred in the region. Artists such as James Taylor, Dizzy Gillespie, Otis Redding, Johnny Mercer, and Travis Tritt prove that musical tastes in these parts are as varied as the landscape.

Bus Travel

Regional bus service, provided by Greyhound, is abundant throughout the Carolinas and Georgia. It's a handy and affordable means of getting around; if it's a simple matter of getting from one city to another, and you've got a bit of time on your hands, consider this option.

Chatham Area Transit (CAT) operates buses in Savannah and Chatham County Monday through Saturday from 6 AM to 11 PM, Sunday from 9 to 7. Some lines may stop running earlier or may not run on Sunday. The CAT Shuttle operates throughout the Historic District; the cost is 75¢ one-way. Buses require 75¢ in exact change.

Charleston Area Regional Transit Authority (CARTA) runs buses on routes that cover most of Charleston from 5:35 AM until 10 PM, until 1 AM in and to North Charleston. The cost is $1 (free transfers). DASH (Downtown Area Shuttle) trolley-style buses provide fast service in the main downtown areas. A single fare is $1; $3 is the cost of an all-day pass.

CUTTING COSTS

Greyhound offers the **North America Discovery Pass,** which allows unlimited travel in the United States within any 7-, 10-, 15-, 21-, 30-, 45-, or 60-day period ($199–$549, depending on length of the pass), and the similar International Ameripass (for non–U.S. residents only), which offers 4- to 60-day passes for $135–$494. Greyhound also has senior citizen, children's, and student discounts.

►**BUS INFORMATION: CARTA** (tel. 843/724–7420). **Chatham Area Transit** (tel. 912/233–5767, www.catchacat.org). **Greyhound** (tel. 800/231–2222, www.greyhound.com).

Business Hours

Banks are usually open weekdays from 9 to 4 and some Saturday mornings, the post office from 8 to 5 weekdays and often on Saturday morning. Shops in urban and suburban areas, particularly in indoor and strip malls, typically open at 9 or 10 daily and stay open until anywhere from 6 PM to 10 PM on weekdays and Saturday, and until 5 or 6 on Sunday. Hours vary greatly, so call ahead when in doubt.

Cameras and Photography

The *Kodak Guide to Shooting Great Travel Pictures* (available at bookstores everywhere) is loaded with tips.

►**PHOTO HELP: Kodak Information Center** (tel. 800/242–2424).

EQUIPMENT PRECAUTIONS

Don't pack film and equipment in checked luggage, where it is much more susceptible to damage. X-ray machines used to view checked luggage are becoming much more powerful and therefore are much more likely to ruin your film. Always **keep film and tape out of the sun.** Carry an extra supply of batteries, and **be prepared to turn on your camera or camcorder** to prove to security personnel that the device is real. Always **ask for hand inspection of film,** which becomes clouded after repeated exposure to airport X-ray machines, and **keep videotapes away from metal detectors.**

SURCHARGES

Before you pick up a car in one city and leave it in another, **ask about drop-off charges or one-way service fees,** which can be substantial. Note, too, that some rental agencies charge extra if you return the car before the time specified in your contract. To avoid a hefty refueling fee, **fill the tank just before you turn in the car,** but be aware that gas stations near the rental outlet may overcharge.

Car Travel

Savannah and Charleston can be explored fairly easily on foot or by using public transit and cabs, but a car is helpful to reach many of the most intriguing nearby museums, parks, restaurants, and lodgings. You can get by without a car on Jekyll Island and Sea Island, but you'll need one on St. Simons. You cannot bring a car to Cumberland Island or Little St. Simons.

I-95 slices north–south along the eastern seaboard, intersecting 10 mi west of town with east–west I-16, which dead-ends in downtown Savannah. U.S. 17, the Coastal Highway, also runs north–south through town. U.S. 80, which connects the Atlantic to the Pacific, is another east–west route through Savannah.

I-26 traverses South Carolina from northwest to southeast and terminates at Charleston. U.S. 17, the coast road, passes through Charleston. I-526, also called the Mark Clark Expressway, runs primarily east–west, connecting the West Ashley area to Mount Pleasant.

RULES OF THE ROAD

State lawmakers now set speed limits, even for federal interstate highways. Limits vary from state to state and from rural to urban areas, so **check posted speeds frequently.**

Always **strap young children into approved child-safety seats.**

Children in Savannah and Charleston

This is an enjoyable part of the country for family road trips, and things are relatively affordable—you'll have no problem finding inexpensive kid-friendly hotels and family-style restaurants. Just keep in mind that a number of fine, antiques-filled B&Bs and inns punctuate the landscape, and these places are less suitable for kids—some of them flat-out refuse to accommodate children. Also, some of the quieter and more rural parts of the region—although exuding history—lack child-oriented attractions.

If you are renting a car, don't forget to **arrange for a car seat** when you reserve. For general advice about traveling with children consult Fodor's FYI: *Travel with Your Baby* (available in bookstores everywhere).

FLYING
If your children are two or older, **ask about children's airfares.** As a general rule, infants under two not occupying a seat fly at greatly reduced fares or even for free.

Experts agree that it's a good idea to use safety seats aloft for children weighing less than 40 pounds. Airlines set their own policies: U.S. carriers usually require that the child be ticketed, even if he or she is young enough to ride free, since the seats must be strapped into regular seats. Do **check your airline's policy about using safety seats during takeoff and landing.** And since safety seats are not allowed everywhere in the plane, get your seat assignments early.

When reserving, **request children's meals or a freestanding bassinet** if you need them. But note that bulkhead seats, where you must sit to use the bassinet, may lack an overhead bin or storage space on the floor.

LODGING

Most hotels in South Carolina and Georgia allow children under a certain age to stay in their parents' room at no extra charge, but others charge for them as extra adults; be sure to **find out the cutoff age for children's discounts.**

SIGHTS AND ATTRACTIONS

Places that are especially appealing to children are indicated by a rubber-duckie icon (🐤) in the margin.

Consumer Protection

Whenever shopping or buying travel services in Savannah and Charleston, **pay with a major credit card,** if possible, so you can cancel payment or get reimbursed if there's a problem. If you're doing business with a particular company for the first time, **contact your local Better Business Bureau and the attorney general's offices** in your state and (for U.S. businesses) the company's home state as well. Have any complaints been filed? Finally, if you're buying a package or tour, always **consider travel insurance** that includes default coverage (☞ Insurance).

➤**BBBS: Council of Better Business Bureaus** (4200 Wilson Blvd., Suite 800, Arlington, VA 22203, tel. 703/276–0100, fax 703/525–8277, www.bbb.org).

Customs and Duties

IN AUSTRALIA

Australian residents who are 18 or older may bring home $A400 worth of souvenirs and gifts (including jewelry), 250 cigarettes or 250 grams of tobacco, and 1,125 ml of alcohol (including wine, beer, and spirits). Residents under 18 may bring back $A200 worth of goods. Prohibited items include meat products. Seeds, plants, and fruits need to be declared upon arrival.

➤**INFORMATION: Australian Customs Service** (Regional Director, Box 8, Sydney, NSW 2001; tel. 02/9213–2000 or 1300/363263; 1800/020504 for quarantine-inquiry line; fax 02/9213–4043; www.customs.gov.au).

IN CANADA

Canadian residents who have been out of Canada for at least seven days may bring home C$750 worth of goods duty-free. If you've been away fewer than seven days but more than 48 hours, the duty-free allowance drops to C$200; if your trip lasts 24–48 hours, the allowance is C$50. You may not pool allowances with family members. Goods claimed under the C$750 exemption may follow you by mail; those claimed under the lesser exemptions must accompany you. Alcohol and tobacco products may be included in the seven-day and 48-hour exemptions but not in the 24-hour exemption. If you meet the age requirements of the province or territory through which you reenter Canada, you may bring in, duty-free, 1.14 liters (40 imperial ounces) of wine or liquor or 24 12-ounce cans or bottles of beer or ale. If you are 19 or older you may bring in, duty-free, 200 cigarettes and 50 cigars. Check ahead of time with the Canada Customs Revenue Agency or the Department of Agriculture for policies regarding meat products, seeds, plants, and fruits.

You may send an unlimited number of gifts worth up to C$60 each duty-free to Canada. Label the package UNSOLICITED GIFT—VALUE UNDER $60. Alcohol and tobacco are excluded.

➤**INFORMATION: Canada Customs and Revenue Agency** (2265 St. Laurent Blvd. S, Ottawa, Ontario K1G 4K3, tel. 204/983–3500, 506/636–5064, 800/461–9999, www.ccra-adrc.gc.ca/).

IN NEW ZEALAND

Homeward-bound residents 17 or older may bring back $700 worth of souvenirs and gifts. Your duty-free allowance also includes 4.5 liters of wine or beer; one 1,125-ml bottle of spirits; and either 200 cigarettes, 250 grams of tobacco, 50 cigars, or a combination of the three up to 250 grams. Prohibited items include meat products, seeds, plants, and fruits.

➤**INFORMATION: New Zealand Customs** (Head office: The Customhouse, 17–21 Whitmore St., Box 2218, Wellington, tel. 09/300–5399 or 0800/428–786, www.customs.govt.nz).

IN THE U.K.

From countries outside the European Union, including the United States, you may bring home, duty-free, 200 cigarettes or 50 cigars; 1 liter of spirits or 2 liters of fortified or sparkling wine or liqueurs; 2 liters of still table wine; 60 milliliters of perfume; 250 milliliters of toilet water; plus £145 worth of other goods, including gifts and souvenirs. If returning from outside the EU, prohibited items include meat products, seeds, plants, and fruits.

➤**INFORMATION: HM Customs and Excise** (Dorset House, Stamford St., Bromley, Kent BR1 1XX, U.K., tel. 020/7202–4227, www.hmce.gov.uk).

Dining

The restaurants listed are the cream of the crop in each price category. They are indicated in the text by a icon. Properties indicated by a icon are lodging establishments whose restaurant warrants a special trip.

RESERVATIONS AND DRESS

Reservations are always a good idea: they are mentioned only when they're essential or not accepted. Book as far ahead as you can, and reconfirm as soon as you arrive. Dress is only mentioned when men are required to wear a jacket or a jacket and tie.

Disabilities and Accessibility

Savannah and Charleston rank on a par with the rest of America in their accessibility for persons with disabilities or special needs. A drawback is the abundance of historic accommodations, restaurants, and attractions with narrow staircases, doorways, and small rooms that fail to conform to the Americans with Disabilities Act (ADA) guidelines. Increasingly, however, businesses throughout the region—especially those in densely populated areas—are changing to improve accessibility.

RESERVATIONS

When discussing accessibility with an operator or reservations agent, **ask hard questions.** Are there any stairs, inside or out? Are there grab bars next to the toilet *and* in the shower/tub? How wide is the doorway to the room? To the bathroom? For the most extensive facilities meeting the latest legal specifications, **opt for newer accommodations.**

➤**COMPLAINTS: Aviation Consumer Protection Division** (☞ Air Travel) for airline-related problems. **Departmental Office of Civil Rights** (for general inquiries, U.S. Department of Transportation, S-30, 400 7th St. SW, Room 10215, Washington, DC 20590, tel. 202/366–4648, fax 202/366–3571, www.dot.gov/ost/docr/index.htm). **Disability Rights Section** (NYAV, U.S. Department of Justice, Civil Rights Division, 950 Pennsylvania Ave. NW, Washington, DC 20530, tel. 202/514–0301 for ADA information line; 800/514–0301; 202/514–0383 for TTY; 800/514–0383 for TTY, www.usdoj.gov/crt/ada/adahom1.htm).

TRAVEL AGENCIES

In the United States, the Americans with Disabilities Act requires that travel firms serve the needs of all travelers. Some agencies specialize in working with people with disabilities.

➤**TRAVELERS WITH MOBILITY PROBLEMS: Access Adventures** (206 Chestnut Ridge Rd., Scottsville, NY 14624, tel. 716/889–9096), run by a former physical-rehabilitation counselor. **Accessible Vans of America** (9 Spielman Rd., Fairfield, NJ 07004, tel. 877/282–8267, fax 973/808–9713, www.accessiblevans.com). **CareVacations** (No. 5, 5110–50 Ave., Leduc, Alberta T9E 6V4, Canada, tel. 780/986–6404 or 877/478–7827, fax 780/986–8332, www.carevacations.com), for group tours and cruise vacations. **Flying Wheels Travel** (143 W. Bridge St., Box 382, Owatonna, MN 55060, tel. 507/451–5005, fax 507/451–1685, www.flyingwheelstravel.com).

Discounts and Deals

Be a smart shopper and compare all your options before making decisions. A plane ticket bought with a promotional coupon from travel clubs, coupon books, and direct-mail offers or on the Internet may not be cheaper than the least expensive fare from a discount ticket agency. And always keep in mind that what you get is just as important as what you save.

DISCOUNT RESERVATIONS

To save money, look into discount reservations services with toll-free numbers, which use their buying power to get a better price on hotels, airline tickets, even car rentals. When booking a room, always call the hotel's local toll-free number (if one is available) rather than the central reservations number—you'll often get a better price. Always ask about special packages or corporate rates.

➤AIRLINE TICKETS: tel. 800/FLY–ASAP.

➤HOTEL ROOMS: **Accommodations Express** (tel. 800/444–7666, www.accommodationsexpress.com). **Central Reservation Service (CRS)** (tel. 800/548–3311, www.roomconnection.net). **Hotel Reservations Network** (tel. 800/964–6835, www.hoteldiscount.com). **Players Express Vacations** (tel. 800/458–6161, www.playersexpress.com). **Quikbook** (tel. 800/789–9887, www.quikbook.com). **RMC**

Travel (tel. 800/245–5738, www.rmcwebtravel.com). **Steigenberger Reservation Service** (tel. 800/223–5652, www.srs-worldhotels.com). **Turbotrip.com** (tel. 800/473–7829, www.turbotrip.com).

PACKAGE DEALS
Don't confuse packages and guided tours. When you buy a package, you travel on your own, just as though you had planned the trip yourself. Fly/drive packages, which combine airfare and car rental, are often a good deal.

Emergencies

Candler Hospital and Memorial Health University Medical Center are Savannah-area hospitals with 24-hour emergency rooms. In Charleston the emergency rooms are open all night at Charleston Memorial Hospital, MUSC Hospital, and Roper Hospital.

➤**EMERGENCY SERVICES: Ambulance, police** (tel. 911).

➤**HOSPITALS: Candler Hospital** (5353 Reynolds St., Kensington Park, tel. 912/692–6000). **Charleston Memorial Hospital** (326 Calhoun St., Upper King, tel. 843/577–0600). **Memorial Health University Medical Center** (4700 Waters Ave., Fairfield, tel. 912/350–8000). **MUSC Hospital** (169 Ashley Ave., Upper King, tel. 843/792–3826). **Roper Hospital** (316 Calhoun St., Upper King, tel. 843/724–2000).

➤**24-HOUR PHARMACIES: CVS Pharmacy** (Medical Arts Shopping Center, 4725 Waters Ave., Fairfield, tel. 912/355–7111).

➤**LATE-NIGHT PHARMACIES: CVS Pharmacy** (Medical Arts Shopping Center, 4725 Waters Ave., Savannah, GA, tel. 912/355–7111). **Eckerds** (Calhoun St. and Rutledge Ave., Upper King, Charleston, SC, tel. 843/805–6022).

Gay and Lesbian Travel

Attitudes about gays and lesbians tend toward the disapproving in some parts of the South, especially outside urban areas. On the whole, however, despite a reputation for conservative-minded residents, this part of the country is not any more hostile or dangerous for lesbians and gays—traveling solo or together—than the rest of America. In fact, you'll find thriving gay communities in Savannah and Charleston. For details about the gay and lesbian scene, consult *Fodor's Gay Guide to the USA* (available in bookstores everywhere). The book provides information on the gay scenes in Asheville, Atlanta, Charleston, Charlotte, Raleigh–Durham, and Savannah.

➤**GAY- AND LESBIAN-FRIENDLY TRAVEL AGENCIES:** **Different Roads Travel** (8383 Wilshire Blvd., Suite 902, Beverly Hills, CA 90211, tel. 323/651–5557 or 800/429–8747, fax 323/651–3678). **Kennedy Travel** (314 Jericho Turnpike, Floral Park, NY 11001, tel. 516/352–4888 or 800/237–7433, fax 516/354–8849, www.kennedytravel.com). **Now, Voyager** (4406 18th St., San Francisco, CA 94114, tel. 415/626–1169 or 800/255–6951, fax 415/626–8626, www.nowvoyager.com). **Skylink Travel and Tour** (1006 Mendocino Ave., Santa Rosa, CA 95401, tel. 707/546–9888 or 800/225–5759, fax 707/546–9891), serving lesbian travelers.

Guidebooks

Plan well, and you won't be sorry. Guidebooks are excellent tools—and you can take them with you. *Fodor's Road Guide USA: Georgia, North Carolina, South Carolina* provides listings of thousands of sights, motels and hotels, and restaurants throughout the region. *Compass American Guides: Georgia* and *Compass American Guides: South Carolina*, with their handsome photos and historical, cultural, and topical essays, are good companions to this guide.

Health

PESTS AND OTHER HAZARDS

Mosquitoes, seasonal black flies, and other insects known to North America proliferate in the humid and often lush Southern states. **Exercise common precautions and wear lotions or sprays that keep away such pests.**

Holidays

Major national holidays include New Year's Day (Jan. 1); Martin Luther King, Jr., Day (3rd Mon. in Jan.); President's Day (3rd Mon. in Feb.); Memorial Day (last Mon. in May); Independence Day (July 4); Labor Day (1st Mon. in Sept.); Thanksgiving Day (4th Thurs. in Nov.); Christmas Eve and Christmas Day (Dec. 24 and 25); and New Year's Eve (Dec. 31).

Insurance

The most useful travel-insurance plan is a comprehensive policy that includes coverage for trip cancellation and interruption, default, trip delay, and medical expenses (with a waiver for preexisting conditions).

Without insurance you will lose all or most of your money if you cancel your trip, regardless of the reason. Default insurance covers you if your tour operator, airline, or cruise line goes out of business. Trip-delay covers expenses that arise because of bad weather or mechanical delays. Study the fine print when comparing policies.

Always **buy travel policies directly from the insurance company**; if you buy them from a cruise line, airline, or tour operator that goes out of business you probably will not be covered for the agency or operator's default, a major risk. Before making any purchase, **review your existing health and home-owner's policies** to find what they cover away from home.

If you are traveling from outside the United States or Canada, *see* Insurance in For International Travelers.

➤**TRAVEL INSURERS: Access America** (6600 W. Broad St., Richmond, VA 23230, tel. 800/284–8300, fax 804/673–1491 or 800/346–9265, www.accessamerica.com). **Travel Guard International** (1145 Clark St., Stevens Point, WI 54481, tel. 715/345–0505 or 800/826–1300, fax 800/955–8785, www. travelguard.com).

For International Travelers

For information on customs restrictions, *see* Customs and Duties.

CAR TRAVEL
In South Carolina and Georgia gasoline costs $.90–$1.25 a gallon. Stations are plentiful. Most stay open late (24 hours along large highways and in big cities), except in rural areas, where Sunday hours are limited and where you may drive long stretches without a refueling opportunity. Highways are well paved. The fastest routes are interstate highways—limited-access multilane highways whose numbers are prefixed by "I–." Interstates with three-digit numbers encircle or intersect urban areas, which may have other limited-access expressways, freeways, and parkways as well. Tolls may be levied on limited-access highways. So-called U.S. highways and state highways are not necessarily limited access, but many have several lanes. Along larger highways roadside stops with rest rooms, fast-food restaurants, and sundries stores are well spaced. State police and tow trucks patrol major highways and lend assistance. If your car breaks down on an interstate, pull onto the shoulder and wait for help, or have your passengers wait while you walk to an emergency phone. If you carry a cell phone, dial *55, noting your location on the small green roadside mileage markers.

Driving in the United States is on the right. Do **obey speed limits** posted along roads and highways. Watch for lower limits in small towns and on back roads. Georgia and South Carolina require front-seat passengers to wear seat belts. On weekdays between 6 AM and 10 AM and again between 4 PM and 7 PM **expect heavy traffic.** To encourage carpooling, some freeways have special lanes for what are designated high-occupancy vehicles (HOV)—cars carrying more than one passenger.

Bookstores, gas stations, convenience stores, and rest stops sell maps ($3–$5) and multiregion road atlases ($10 and up).

CONSULATES AND EMBASSIES
➤**AUSTRALIA: Australian Embassy** (1601 Massachusetts Ave. NW, Washington, DC 20036, tel. 202/797–3000).

➤**CANADA: Canadian Embassy** (501 Pennsylvania Ave. NW, Washington, DC 20001, tel. 202/682–1740).

➤**NEW ZEALAND: New Zealand Embassy** (37 Observatory Circle NW, Washington, DC 20008, tel. 202/328–4800).

➤**UNITED KINGDOM: British Embassy** (19 Observatory Circle NW, Washington, DC 20008, tel. 202/588–7800).

CURRENCY
The dollar is the basic unit of U.S. currency. It has 100 cents. Coins include the copper penny (1¢); the silvery nickel (5¢), dime (10¢), quarter (25¢), and half-dollar (50¢); and the golden $1 coin, replacing a now-rare silver dollar. Bills are denominated $1, $5, $10, $20, $50, and $100, all green and identical in size; designs vary. The exchange rate at press time was US$1.58 per British pound, 64¢ per Canadian dollar, 54¢ per Australian dollar, and 46¢ per New Zealand dollar.

ELECTRICITY
The U.S. standard is AC, 110 volts/60 cycles. Plugs have two flat pins set parallel to each other.

EMERGENCIES

For police, fire, or ambulance, **dial 911** (0 in rural areas).

INSURANCE

Britons and Australians need extra medical coverage when traveling overseas.

➤**INSURANCE INFORMATION: In the U.K.: Association of British Insurers** (51–55 Gresham St., London EC2V 7HQ, U.K., tel. 020/7600–3333, fax 020/7696–8999, www.abi.org.uk). In Australia: **Insurance Council of Australia** (Level 3, 56 Pitt St., Sydney NSW 2000, tel. 02/9253–5100, fax 02/9253–5111, www.ica.com.au). In Canada: **RBC Insurance** (6880 Financial Dr., Mississauga, Ontario L5N 7Y5, Canada, tel. 905/816–2400 or 800/668–4342 in Canada, fax 905/816–2498, www.royalbank.com). In New Zealand: **Insurance Council of New Zealand** (Box 474, Wellington, New Zealand, tel. 04/472–5230, fax 04/473–3011, www.icnz.org.nz).

MAIL AND SHIPPING

You can buy stamps and aerograms and send letters and parcels in post offices. Stamp-dispensing machines can occasionally be found in airports, bus and train stations, office buildings, drugstores, and the like. You can also deposit mail in the stout, dark blue, steel bins at strategic locations everywhere and in the mail chutes of large buildings; pickup schedules are posted.

For mail sent within the United States, you need a 37¢ stamp for first-class letters weighing up to 1 ounce (23¢ for each additional ounce) and 23¢ for postcards. You pay 80¢ for 1-ounce airmail letters and 70¢ for airmail postcards to most other countries; for mail to Canada and Mexico you need a 60¢ stamp for a 1-ounce letter and 50¢ for a postcard. An aerogram—a single sheet of lightweight blue paper that folds into its own envelope, stamped for overseas airmail—costs 70¢.

To receive mail on the road, have it sent c/o General Delivery at your destination's main post office (use the correct five-digit zip code). You must pick up mail in person within 30 days and show a driver's license or passport.

PASSPORTS AND VISAS

When traveling internationally, **carry your passport** even if you don't need one (it's always the best form of I.D.) and **make two photocopies of the data page** (one for someone at home and another for you, carried separately from your passport). If you lose your passport, promptly call the nearest embassy or consulate and the local police.

Visitor visas are not necessary for Canadian citizens, or for citizens of Australia and the United Kingdom who are staying fewer than 90 days.

➤**AUSTRALIAN CITIZENS: Australian State Passport Office** (tel. 131–232, www.passports.gov.au).

➤**CANADIAN CITIZENS: Passport Office** (tel. 819/994–3500 or 800/567–6868 in Canada; www.dfait-maeci.gc.ca/passport).

➤**NEW ZEALAND CITIZENS: New Zealand Passport Office** (tel. 04/474–8100 for application procedures, 0800/22–5050 in New Zealand for application-status updates; www.passports.govt.nz).

➤**U.K. CITIZENS: London Passport Office** (tel. 0870/521–0410, www.passport.gov.uk). **U.S. Embassy** (enclose a SASE to Consular Information Unit, 24 Grosvenor Sq., London W1 1AE, for general information; Visa Branch, 5 Upper Grosvenor St., London W1A 2JB, to submit an application via mail; tel. 09068/200–290 for recorded visa information with per-minute charges; www.usembassy.org.uk).

TELEPHONES

All U.S. telephone numbers consist of a three-digit area code and a seven-digit local number. Within many local calling areas, dial only the seven-digit number; but in larger cities or regions with more than one area code (such as Atlanta and Charlotte), dial "1" then all 10 digits whether for local or long-distance calls. To call between area-code regions, dial "1" then all 10 digits; the same goes for calls to numbers prefixed by "800," "888," "877," and "866"—all toll-free. For calls to numbers preceded by "900" you must pay—usually dearly.

For international calls, dial "011" followed by the country code and the local number. For help, dial "0" and ask for an overseas operator. The country code is 61 for Australia, 64 for New Zealand, 44 for the United Kingdom. Calling Canada is the same as calling within the United States. Most local phone books list country codes and U.S. area codes. The country code for the United States is 1.

For operator assistance, dial "0." To obtain someone's phone number, call directory assistance, 555–1212 or occasionally 411 (free at some public phones). To have the person you're calling foot the bill, phone collect; dial "0" instead of "1" before the 10-digit number.

At pay phones, instructions are usually posted. Usually you insert coins in a slot (25¢–50¢ for local calls) and wait for a steady tone before dialing. When you call long-distance, the operator will tell you how much to insert; prepaid phone cards, widely available in various denominations, are easier. Call the number on the back, punch in the card's personal identification number when prompted, then dial your number.

For more information on area codes and making long-distance calls, *see* Telephones.

Lodging

All major chains are well represented in this part of the country, both in cities and suburbs, and interstates are lined with inexpensive to moderate chains. It's not uncommon to find clean but extremely basic discount chains offering double rooms for as little as $25 to $40 nightly along the busiest highways.

In cities and some large towns you might want to forgo a modern hotel in favor of a historic property—there are dozens of fine old hotels, many of them fully restored and quite a few offering better rates than chain properties with comparable amenities and nowhere near the style.

The lodgings listed are the cream of the crop in each price category. They are denoted in the text by a icon; lodging establishments whose restaurant warrants a special trip are denoted by a icon. Facilities that are available are listed—but not any extra costs associated with those facilities. When pricing accommodations, **always ask what's included and what costs extra.**

Assume that hotels operate on the **European Plan** (EP, with no meals) unless it is specified that they use the **Continental Plan** (CP, with a Continental breakfast), **Breakfast Plan** (BP, with a full breakfast), **Modified American Plan** (MAP, with breakfast and dinner), or the **Full American Plan** (FAP, with all meals).

APARTMENT AND VILLA RENTALS

If you want a home base that's roomy enough for a family and comes with cooking facilities, **consider a furnished rental.** These can save you money, especially if you're traveling with a group. Home-exchange directories sometimes list rentals as well as exchanges.

In Charleston, rates tend to increase and reservations are essential during both the Spring Festival of Houses and Spoleto. For historic home rentals in Charleston, contact Charleston Carriage Houses–Oceanfront Realty. For condo and house rentals on Kiawah Island, Sullivan's Island, and the Isle of

Palms—some with private pools and tennis courts—try Great Beach Vacations.

➤**INTERNATIONAL AGENTS: Hideaways International** (767 Islington St., Portsmouth, NH 03801, tel. 603/430–4433 or 800/843–4433, fax 603/430–4444, www.hideaways.com; membership $129). **Vacation Home Rentals Worldwide** (235 Kensington Ave., Norwood, NJ 07648, tel. 201/767–9393 or 800/633–3284, fax 201/767–5510, www.vhrww.com).

➤**LOCAL AGENTS: Great Beach Vacations** (1517 Palm Blvd., Isle of Palms 29451, tel. 843/886–9704). **Charleston Carriage Houses–Oceanfront Realty** (Box 6151, Hilton Head 29938, tel. 843/785–8161).

BED-AND-BREAKFASTS AND INNS

To find rooms in homes, cottages, and carriage houses, try Historic Charleston Bed and Breakfast. Southern Hospitality B&B Reservations handles rooms in homes and carriage houses.

➤**RESERVATION SERVICES: Historic Charleston Bed and Breakfast** (60 Broad St., South of Broad, Charleston 29401, tel. 843/722–6606). **Southern Hospitality B&B Reservations** (110 Amelia Dr., Lexington 29072, tel. 843/356–6238 or 800/374–7422).

HOME EXCHANGES

If you would like to exchange your home for someone else's, **join a home-exchange organization,** which will send you its updated listings of available exchanges for a year and will include your own listing in at least one of them. It's up to you to make specific arrangements.

➤**EXCHANGE CLUBS: HomeLink International** (Box 47747, Tampa, FL 33647, tel. 813/975–9825 or 800/638–3841, fax 813/910–8144, www.homelink.org; $98 per year). **Intervac U.S.** (30 Corte San Fernando, Tiburon, CA 94920, tel. 800/756–4663, fax 415/435-7440, www.intervacus.com; $90 yearly fee for a listing, on-line access, and a catalog; $50 without catalog).

HOSTELS

No matter what your age, you can **save on lodging costs by staying at hostels**. In some 4,500 locations in more than 70 countries around the world, Hostelling International (HI), the umbrella group for a number of national youth-hostel associations, offers single-sex, dorm-style beds and, at many hostels, rooms for couples and family accommodations. Membership in any HI national hostel association, open to travelers of all ages, allows you to stay in HI-affiliated hostels at member rates; one-year membership is about $25 for adults (C$26.75 in Canada, £13 in the U.K., $A52 in Australia, and NZ$40 in New Zealand); hostels run about $10 to $30 per night. Members have priority if the hostel is full; they're also eligible for discounts around the world, even on rail and bus travel in some countries.

➤ORGANIZATIONS: **Hostelling International—American Youth Hostels** (733 15th St. NW, Suite 840, Washington, DC 20005, tel. 202/783-6161, fax 202/783-6171, www.hiayh.org). **Hostelling International—Canada** (400-205 Catherine St., Ottawa, Ontario K2P 1C3, Canada, tel. 613/237-7884 or 800/663-5777, fax 613/237-7868, www.hostellingintl.ca). **Youth Hostel Association of England and Wales** (Trevelyan House, Dimple Rd., Matlock, Derbyshire DE4 3YH, tel. 0870/870-8808, fax 0169/592-702, www.yha.org.uk). **Australian Youth Hostel Association** (10 Mallett St., Camperdown, NSW 2050, Australia, tel. 02/9565-1699, fax 02/9565-1325, www.yha.com.au). **Youth Hostels Association of New Zealand** (Level 3, 193 Cashel St., Box 436, Christchurch, tel. 03/379-9970, fax 03/365-4476, www.yha.org.nz).

HOTELS

All hotels listed have private bath unless otherwise noted.

➤**TOLL-FREE NUMBERS: Adam's Mark** (tel. 800/444–2326, www.adamsmark.com). **Baymont Inns** (tel. 800/428–3438, www.baymontinns.com). **Best Western** (tel. 800/528–1234, www.bestwestern.com). **Choice** (tel. 800/424–6423, www.choicehotels.com). **Clarion** (tel. 800/424–6423, www.choicehotels.com). **Colony** (tel. 800/777–1700). **Comfort Inn** (tel. 800/424–6423, www.choicehotels.com). **Days Inn** (tel. 800/325–2525, www.daysinn.com). **Doubletree and Red Lion Hotels** (tel. 800/222–8733, www.hilton.com). **Embassy Suites** (tel. 800/362–2779, www.embassysuites.com). **Fairfield Inn** (tel. 800/228–2800, www.marriott.com). **Four Seasons** (tel. 800/332–3442, www.fourseasons.com). **Hilton** (tel. 800/445–8667, www.hilton.com). **Holiday Inn** (tel. 800/465–4329, www.sixcontinentshotels.com). **Howard Johnson** (tel. 800/654–4656, www.hojo.com). **Hyatt Hotels & Resorts** (tel. 800/233–1234, www.hyatt.com). **La Quinta** (tel. 800/531–5900, www.laquinta.com). **Marriott** (tel. 800/228–9290, www.marriott.com). **Omni** (tel. 800/843–6664, www.omnihotels.com). **Quality Inn** (tel. 800/424–6423, www.choicehotels.com). **Radisson** (tel. 800/333–3333, www.radisson.com). **Ramada** (tel. 800/228–2828, www.ramada.com). **Renaissance Hotels & Resorts** (tel. 800/468–3571, www.renaissancehotels.com/). **Ritz-Carlton** (tel. 800/241–3333, www.ritzcarlton.com). **Sheraton** (tel. 800/325–3535, www.starwood.com). **Westin Hotels & Resorts** (tel. 800/228–3000, www.westin.com). **Wyndham Hotels & Resorts** (tel. 800/822–4200, www.wyndham.com).

MOTELS
➤**TOLL-FREE NUMBERS: Budget Hosts Inns** (tel. 800/283–4678). **Econo Lodge** (tel. 800/553–2666, www.econolodge.com). **Friendship Inns** (tel. 800/453–4511). **Motel 6** (tel. 800/466–8356, www.motel6.com). **Rodeway** (tel. 800/228–2000, www.rodeway.com). **Super 8** (tel. 800/848–8888, www.super8.com).

Media

NEWSPAPERS AND MAGAZINES

There's no major regional newspaper that serves the area, but just about every city with a population of greater than 40,000 or 50,000 also publishes its own daily paper.

Most major cities have very good alternative newsweeklies with useful Web sites and information on area dining, arts, and sightseeing—these are usually free and found in restaurants, coffeehouses, bookstores, tourism offices, hotel lobbies, and some nightclubs. Of particular note is Atlanta's *Creative Loafing*, which has separate editions for a number of additional Southern cities. Visit its Web site (www.cln.com) to find links to other useful alternative newsweeklies in Savannah and Charleston.

The monthly features magazine *Southern Living* gives a nice sense of travel, food, and lifestyle issues relevant to the region. Local lifestyles magazines serve Savannah and Charleston. These publications have colorful stories and dining and entertainment coverage; they're worth picking up prior to your visit, especially if you're planning an extended stay; virtually all of these have useful Web sites, too.

RADIO AND TELEVISION

All the major television and radio networks have local affiliates and channels throughout the Carolinas and Georgia.

Money Matters

As with most of America, credit and debit cards are accepted at the vast majority of shops, sit-down restaurants, and accommodations in Savannah and Charleston. Common exceptions include small, independent stores. Banks—as well as convenience stores, groceries, and even nightclubs—with ATMs are easy to find in just about every community.

Although the cost of living remains fairly low in most parts of the South, travel-related costs (such as dining, lodging, museums, and transportation) have become increasingly steep over the years and can be dear in resort communities throughout the Carolinas and Georgia.

Prices throughout this guide are given for adults. Substantially reduced fees are almost always available for children, students, and senior citizens. For information on taxes, *see* Taxes.

CREDIT CARDS

Throughout this guide, the following abbreviations are used: **AE,** American Express; **D,** Discover; **DC,** Diners Club; **MC,** MasterCard; and **V,** Visa.

➤**REPORTING LOST CARDS: American Express** (tel. 800/441–0519). **Diners Club** (tel. 800/234–6377). **Discover** (tel. 800/347–2683). **MasterCard** (tel. 800/622–7747). **Visa** (tel. 800/847–2911).

Packing

Georgia is hot and humid in the summer and sunny and mild in the winter. Smart but casual attire works fine almost everywhere you'll go, with a few exceptions requiring more formal dress. For colder months pack a lightweight coat, slacks, and sweaters; you'll need heavier clothing in some mountainous areas, where cold, damp weather prevails and snow is not unusual. Keeping summer's humidity in mind, **pack absorbent natural fabrics that breathe;** bring an umbrella, but leave the plastic raincoat at home. You'll want a jacket or sweater for summer evenings and for too-cool air-conditioning. And **don't forget insect repellent.**

In your carry-on luggage, **pack an extra pair of eyeglasses or contact lenses and enough of any medication** you take to last a few days longer than the entire trip. You may also ask your doctor to write a spare prescription using the drug's generic name, since brand names may vary from country to country. In luggage to be checked, **never pack prescription drugs or valuables.** To avoid customs delays, carry medications in their original packaging. And don't forget to carry with you the addresses of offices that handle refunds of lost traveler's checks. Check *Fodor's How to Pack* (available in bookstores everywhere) for more tips.

CHECKING LUGGAGE

How many carry-on bags you can bring with you is up to the airline. Most allow two, but not always, so make sure that everything you carry aboard will fit under your seat or in the overhead bin, and get to the gate early. Note that if you have a seat at the back of the plane, you'll probably board first, while the overhead bins are still empty.

If you are flying internationally, note that baggage allowances may be determined not by piece but by weight—generally 88 pounds (40 kilograms) in first class, 66 pounds (30 kilograms) in business class, and 44 pounds (20 kilograms) in economy.

Airline liability for baggage is limited to $1,250 per person on flights within the United States. On international flights it amounts to $9.07 per pound or $20 per kilogram for checked baggage (roughly $640 per 70-pound bag) and $400 per passenger for unchecked baggage. You can buy additional coverage at check-in for about $10 per $1,000 of coverage, but it excludes a rather extensive list of items, shown on your airline ticket.

Before departure, **itemize your bags' contents** and their worth, and label the bags with your name, address, and phone number. (If you use your home address, cover it so potential thieves can't see it readily.) Inside each bag, **pack a copy of your itinerary.** At check-in, **make sure that each bag is correctly tagged** with the destination airport's three-letter code. If your bags arrive damaged or fail to arrive at all, file a written report with the airline before leaving the airport.

Safety

You have little cause of worry about theft or crime—just exercise common sense. Be wary of suspicious-looking figures and keep valuables hidden away or locked up, if possible. Especially in urban areas and along major highways, never leave valuables in your unattended car. Wherever you venture in this part of the world, folks are generally happy to offer directions and advice.

Senior-Citizen Travel

To qualify for age-related discounts, **mention your senior-citizen status up front** when booking hotel reservations (not when checking out) and before you're seated in restaurants (not when paying the bill). When renting a car, ask about promotional car-rental discounts, which can be cheaper than senior-citizen rates.

➤EDUCATIONAL PROGRAMS: Elderhostel (11 Ave. de Lafayette, Boston, MA 02111-1746, tel. 877/426–8056, fax 877/426–2166, www.elderhostel.org).

Sightseeing Tours

SAVANNAH
➤HISTORIC DISTRICT TOURS: Beach Institute African-American Cultural Center (tel. 912/234–8000). Carriage Tours of Savannah (tel. 912/236–6756). Garden Club of Savannah (tel. 912/238–0248). Old Town Trolley Tours (tel. 912/233–0083).

➤SPECIAL-INTEREST TOURS: Gray Line (tel. 912/234–8687 or 800/426–2318). Historic Savannah Foundation (tel. 912/234–4088 or 800/627–5030). Square Routes (tel. 912/232–6866 or 800/868–6867).

➤WALKING TOURS: A Ghost Talk Ghost Walk Tour (Reynolds Sq., Congress and Abercorn Sts., Historic District, tel. 912/

233–3896). **Savannah-By-Foot's Creepy Crawl Haunted Pub Tour** (tel. 912/398–3833). **Six Pence Pub** (245 Bull St., Historic District).

CHARLESTON

➤**BOAT TOURS: Charleston Harbor Tour** (tel. 843/722–1691). **Fort Sumter Tours** (tel. 843/722–1691, 843/881–7337, or 800/789–3678). **Princess Gray Line Harbor Tours** (tel. 843/722–1112 or 800/344–4483).

➤**BUS TOURS: Adventure Sightseeing** (tel. 843/762–0088 or 800/722–5394). **Colonial Coach and Trolley Company** (tel. 843/795–3000). **Doin' the Charleston** (tel. 843/763–1233 or 800/647–4487). **Gray Line** (tel. 843/722–4444).

➤**CARRIAGE TOURS: Lowcountry Carriage Co.** (tel. 843/577–0042). **Old South Carriage Company** (tel. 843/723–9712). **Palmetto Carriage Tours** (tel. 843/723–8145).

➤**SPECIAL-INTEREST TOURS: Chai Y'All** (tel. 843/556–0664). **Flying High over Charleston** (tel. 843/569–6148). **Gullah Tours** (tel. 843/763–7551). **Sweetgrass Tours** (tel. 843/556–0664 for groups).

➤**PRIVATE GUIDES: Associated Guides of Historic Charleston** (tel. 843/724–6419). **Charleston's Finest Historic Tours** (tel. 843/577–3311). **Janice Kahn** (tel. 843/556–0664).

➤**WALKING TOURS: Charleston Strolls** (tel. 843/766–2080). **Charleston Tea Party Walking Tour** (tel. 843/577–5896 or 843/722–1779). **Ghosts of Charleston** (tel. 843/723–1670 or 800/854–1670). **On the Market Tours** (tel. 843/853–8687). **Original Charleston Walks** (tel. 843/577–3800 or 800/729–3420).

Students in Savannah and Charleston

➤**IDS AND SERVICES: STA Travel** (tel. 212/627–3111 or 800/ 781–4040, fax 212/627–3387, www.sta.com). **Travel Cuts** (187 College St., Toronto, Ontario M5T 1P7, Canada, tel. 416/979– 2406 or 800/667–2887 in Canada, fax 416/979–8167, www. travelcuts.com).

Taxes

SALES TAX

Sales taxes are as follows: Georgia 4% and South Carolina 5%. Some counties or cities may impose an additional 1% to 3% tax. Most municipalities also levy a lodging tax (usually exempt at small inns with only a few rooms, but rules vary regionally) and, in some cases, a restaurant tax. The hotel taxes in the South can be rather steep, greater than 10% in Georgia.

Train Travel

Amtrak has regular service along the eastern seaboard, with daily stops in Savannah and Charleston.

➤**TRAIN INFORMATION: Amtrak** (tel. 800/872–7245). **Amtrak Charleston** (4565 Gaynor Ave., North Charleston, tel. 843/744–8264 or 800/872–7245). **Amtrak Savannah** (2611 Seaboard Coastline Dr., Telfair Junction, tel. 912/234–2611 or 800/872–7245, www.amtrak.com).

CUTTING COSTS

Amtrak offers different kinds of rail passes that allow for travel within certain regions, including a set number of stops, at a significant savings over the standard posted fare. They also have a **North American rail pass** that offers you unlimited travel with the United States and Canada within any 30-day period ($674 peak, $475 off-peak). For non–U.S. residents only, they have several kinds of **USA rail passes,** offering unlimited travel for

15–30 days. Amtrak also has senior citizen, children's, disability, and student discounts, as well as occasional deals that allow a second or third accompanying passenger to travel for half price or even free. The **Amtrak Vacations** program customizes entire vacations, including hotels, car rentals, and tours.

Travel Agencies

A good travel agent puts your needs first. Look for an agency that has been in business at least five years, emphasizes customer service, and has someone on staff who specializes in your destination. In addition, **make sure the agency belongs to a professional trade organization.** The American Society of Travel Agents (ASTA), with more than 24,000 members in some 140 countries, is the largest and most influential in the field. Operating under the motto "Without a travel agent, you're on your own," it maintains and enforces a strict code of ethics and will step in to help mediate any agent-client disputes if necessary. ASTA also maintains a Web site that includes a directory of agents. (If a travel agency is also acting as your tour operator, *see* Buyer Beware in Tours and Packages.)

➤**LOCAL AGENT REFERRALS: American Society of Travel Agents** (ASTA; 1101 King St., Suite 200, Alexandria, VA 22314, tel. 800/965–2782 24-hr hot line, fax 703/739–3268, www.astanet.com). **Association of British Travel Agents** (68–71 Newman St., London W1T 3AH, U.K., tel. 020/7637–2444, fax 020/7637–0713, www.abtanet.com). **Association of Canadian Travel Agents** (130 Albert St., Suite 1705, Ottawa, Ontario K1P 5G4, tel. 613/237–3657, fax 613/237–7052, www.acta.ca). **Australian Federation of Travel Agents** (Level 3, 309 Pitt St., Sydney NSW 2000, Australia, tel. 02/9264–3299, fax 02/9264–1085, www.afta.com.au). **Travel Agents' Association of New Zealand** (Level 5, Tourism and Travel House, 79 Boulcott St., Box 1888, Wellington 6001, tel. 04/499–0104, fax 04/499–0827, www.taanz.org.nz).

Visitor Information

For general information and brochures before you go, contact the state tourism bureaus below. In Charleston, check out the "Tips for Tourists" each Saturday in the *Post & Courier*. Georgia has centralized reservations through the Georgia State Parks department (Reservation Resource).

➤**TOURIST INFORMATION: Brunswick and the Golden Isles Visitors Center** (2000 Glynn Ave., Brunswick 31520, tel. 912/264–5337 or 800/933–2627, www.bgivb.com). **Charleston Area Convention and Visitors Bureau** (Box 975, Charleston 29402, tel. 843/853–8000 or 800/868–8118, www.charlestoncvb.com). **Charleston Visitor Center** (375 Meeting St., Upper King).

Georgia Department of Industry, Trade and Tourism (285 Peachtree Center Ave., N.E. Marquis Tower II, Suite 1100, Atlanta, GA 30303, tel. 404/656–3553 or 800/847–4842, fax 404/651–9462, www.georgia.org). **Georgia State Parks** (tel. 800/864–7275 for reservations; 770/398–7275 within metro Atlanta; 404/656–3530 for general park information; www.gastateparks.org).

Historic Charleston Foundation (Box 1120, Charleston 29402, tel. 843/723–1623). **Preservation Society of Charleston** (Box 521, Charleston 29402, tel. 843/722–4630). **Savannah Area Convention & Visitors Bureau** (101 E. Bay St., Historic District, 31401, tel. 912/644–6401 or 877/728–2662, fax 912/944–0468, www.savcvb.com).

South Carolina Department of Parks, Recreation, and Tourism (1205 Pendleton St., Suite 106, Columbia, SC 29201, tel. 803/734–0122 or 888/SC–SMILE, fax 803/734–0138, www.travelsc.com).

Web Sites

Do check out the World Wide Web when planning your trip. You'll find everything from weather forecasts to virtual tours of famous cities. Be sure to **visit Fodors.com** (www.fodors.com), a complete travel-planning site. You can research prices, check out bargains, and book plane tickets, hotel rooms, rental cars, vacation packages, and more. In addition, you can post your pressing questions in the Travel Talk section. Other planning tools include a currency converter and weather reports, and there are loads of links to travel resources.

When to Go

Spring is probably the most attractive season in this part of the United States. Throughout the region the blooming of cherry blossoms is followed by those of azaleas, dogwoods, and camellias from April into May, with apple blossoms blooming in May. Summer can be hot and humid in many areas, but temperatures will be cooler along the coasts or in the mountains. Folk, crafts, art, and music festivals tend to take place in summer, as do sports events. State and local fairs are held mainly in August and September, although there are a few as early as the first part of July and as late as October. Fall can be a delight, with spectacular foliage, particularly in the mountains.

CLIMATE

In winter temperatures generally average in the low 40s inland, in the 60s by the shore. Summer temperatures, modified by mountains in some areas, by water in others, range from the high 70s to the mid-80s and now and then the low 90s.

▶**FORECASTS: Weather Channel Connection** (tel. 900/932–8437), 95¢ per minute from a Touch-Tone phone.

The following are average daily maximum and minimum temperatures for Savannah and Charleston.

SAVANNAH, GEORGIA

Jan.	59F	15C	May	84F	29C	Sept.	85F	29C
	41	6		62	17		67	19
Feb.	62F	17C	June	88F	31C	Oct.	77F	25C
	41	5		69	21		56	16
Mar.	70F	21C	July	91F	33C	Nov.	70F	21C
	48	9		72	22		48	9
Apr.	77F	25C	Aug.	89F	32C	Dec.	62F	17C
	54	12		72	22		41	5

CHARLESTON, SOUTH CAROLINA

Jan.	59F	15C	May	81F	27C	Sept.	84F	29C
	41	6		64	18		69	21
Feb.	60F	16C	June	86F	30C	Oct.	76F	24C
	43	7		71	22		59	15
Mar.	66F	19C	July	88F	31C	Nov.	67F	19C
	49	9		74	23		49	9
Apr.	73F	23C	Aug.	88F	31C	Dec.	59F	11C
	56	13		73	23		42	6

index

Fodor's
Key to the Guides

America's guidebook leader publishes guides for every kind of traveler. Check out our many series and find your perfect match.

Fodor's Gold Guides

America's favorite travel-guide series offers the most detailed insider reviews of hotels, restaurants, and attractions in all price ranges, plus great background information, smart tips, and useful maps.

Fodor's Road Guide USA

Big guides for a big country—the most comprehensive guides to America's roads, packed with places to stay, eat, and play across the U.S.A. Just right for road warriors, family vacationers, and cross-country trekkers.

COMPASS AMERICAN GUIDES

Stunning guides from top local writers and photographers, with gorgeous photos, literary excerpts, and colorful anecdotes. A must-have for culture mavens, history buffs, and new residents.

Fodor's CITYPACKS

Concise city coverage with a foldout map. The right choice for urban travelers who want everything under one cover.

Fodor's EXPLORING GUIDES

Hundreds of color photos bring your destination to life. Lively stories lend insight into the culture, history, and people.

Fodor's POCKET GUIDES

For travelers who need only the essentials. The best of Fodor's in pocket-size packages for just $9.95.

Fodor's To Go
Credit-card–size, magnetized color microguides that fit in the palm of your hand—perfect for "stealth" travelers or as gifts.

Fodor's FLASHMAPS
Every resident's map guide. 60 easy-to-follow maps of public transit, parks, museums, zip codes, and more.

Fodor's CITYGUIDES
Sourcebooks for living in the city: Thousands of in-the-know listings for restaurants, shops, sports, nightlife, and other city resources.

Fodor's AROUND THE CITY WITH KIDS
68 great ideas for family days, recommended by resident parents. Perfect for exploring in your own backyard or on the road.

Fodor's ESCAPES
Fill your trip with once-in-a-lifetime experiences, from ballooning in Chianti to overnighting in the Moroccan desert. These full-color dream books point the way.

Fodor's FYI
Get tips from the pros on planning the perfect trip. Learn how to pack, fly hassle-free, plan a honeymoon or cruise, stay healthy on the road, and travel with your baby.

Fodor's Languages for Travelers
Practice the local language before hitting the road. Available in phrase books, cassette sets, and CD sets.

Karen Brown's Guides
Engaging guides to the most charming inns and B&Bs in the U.S.A. and Europe, with easy-to-follow inn-to-inn itineraries.

Baedeker's Guides
Comprehensive guides, trusted since 1829, packed with A–Z reviews and star ratings.

FODOR'S POCKET SAVANNAH & CHARLESTON

EDITORS: Nuha Ansari, Diane Mehta, Tom Mercer

Editorial Contributors: Andy Collins, Hollis Gillespie, Mary Sue Lawrence

Editorial Production: Ira-Neil Dittersdorf

Maps: David Lindroth, cartographer; Bob Blake and Rebecca Baer, map editors

Design: Fabrizio La Rocca, creative director; Tigist Getachew, art director; Jolie Novak, senior picture editor; Melanie Marin, photo editor

Production/Manufacturing: Robert B. Shields

Cover Photo: Kunio Owaki/Corbis Stock Market

COPYRIGHT

Fifth Edition

ISBN 1–4000-1209–0

ISSN 1527–3202

IMPORTANT TIP

Although all prices, opening times, and other details in this book are based on information supplied to us at press time, changes occur all the time in the travel world, and Fodor's cannot accept responsibility for facts that become outdated or for inadvertent errors or omissions. So **ALWAYS CONFIRM INFORMATION WHEN IT MATTERS,** especially if you're making a detour to visit a specific place.

SPECIAL SALES

Fodor's Travel Publications are available at special discounts for bulk purchases for sales promotions or premiums. Special editions, including personalized covers, excerpts of existing guides, and corporate imprints, can be created in large quantities for special needs. For more information, contact your local bookseller or write to Special Markets, Fodor's Travel Publications, 1745 Broadway, New York, NY 10019. Inquiries from Canada should be directed to your local Canadian bookseller or sent to Random House of Canada, Ltd., Marketing Department, 2775 Matheson Boulevard East, Mississauga, Ontario L4W 4P7. Inquiries from the United Kingdom should be sent to Fodor's Travel Publications, 20 Vauxhall Bridge Road, London SW1V 2SA, England.

PRINTED IN THE UNITED STATES OF AMERICA

10 9 8 7 6 5 4 3 2 1